TEMPUS
Oral History
SERIES

voices of
GOODISON PARK

A commemorative programme – Everton, FA Cup winners, 1966.

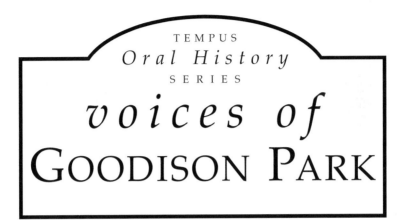

TEMPUS
Oral History
SERIES

voices of
GOODISON PARK

Compiled by
David Paul

TEMPUS

Tempus Publishing Limited
The Mill, Brimscombe Port,
Stroud, Gloucestershire, GL5 2QG

ISBN 0 7524 1548 4

Typesetting and origination by
Tempus Publishing Limited
Printed in Great Britain by
Midway Clark Printing, Wiltshire

For Everton supporters, both past and present – especially my dad and my brother Colin.

CONTENTS

ACKNOWLEDGEMENTS

I would like to thank all the Everton fans who have helped me to write this book, without whom it would not have been possible. I am particularly grateful to Geoff Tinnion for the numerous telephone calls he made on my behalf.

Thanks must also go to the many people who gave me continued assistance, support and guidance. In particular I would like to thank all the supporters who shared their memories with me and who lent their treasured photographs and other mementoes for inclusion in the book:

Dave Alderton, Ray Anderson, Charlie Birch, John Boardman, Steve Bretherton, Stan Cain, Brenda Clintworth, Faye Davies, Ken Davies, Mary Davies, Peter Davies, Paul Durose, Anita Gallagher, Sally Greene, Valerie Grue, Malcolm Hadwin, Linda Harkin, James Harison, Joanne Harison, Joe Harrison, John Harrison, Nick Hawkins, Dave Hughes, Heather Jarvis, Geoff Jones, Dave Kelly, Dolly Kelly, John Kelly, Brian Keoghan, Lin Keoghan, Jim King, Paul Lucas, Larry Lynch, Bob Maylor, John McGovern, Karon Meehan, Yvonne Moogan, Frank Patterson, Colin Paul, Margaret Riding, Tony Riley, Vinny Riley, Lawrence Santangeli, Harold S. Scott, Andrew Skeete, Anthony Skeete, Leo Skeete, Frank Smith, Peter Spear, Joseph Somers, Vincenzo Testaverde, Colin Truesdale, Bob Williams.

And finally, while I have tried to ensure that the stories are factually correct, not easy at the best of times, any errors or inaccuracies are mine alone.

David Paul

INTRODUCTION

In 1888 Everton was one of the founding members of the Football League. In fact, since that time, just about every fact and statistic relating to the club's progress has been documented and chronicled. This book, however, is not full of facts and figures. Its focus is very definitely fixed on the reminiscences and anecdotes of the fans themselves. Throughout the book, fans tell their own stories, some going back fifty years or more. Indeed, one story re-tells and re-lives a Cup game that was played between Everton and Luton in 1933 – the storyteller, John McGovern, still tells it as though it had been played only last week!

In collecting the material for this book, two significant facts were reinforced over and over again. The first is that Everton fans are passionate about their team, and support them through both the good times and the times that are not so good. Secondly, the spirit which has been within Everton right from the early days as St Domingo's Football Club is still alive and well. That spirit and proud tradition have been carried through succeeding teams, by players such as Johnny Holt, Jack Sharp, and Jack Taylor. Later, the mantle was taken by other Everton 'greats' – Cliff Britton and Joe Mercer, right through to Howard Kendall, Alan Ball, Colin Harvey and Peter Reid. There are so many other players that could be mentioned, Tommy Lawton, Fred Pickering, Bob Latchford and Gary Lineker to name but a few. Then, of course, there's one of the greatest football players of all time – in any football team – the legendary Dixie Dean. His outstanding contribution to the club is still talked about in the city and his memory is still cherished.

Although the game of football has been changing over the past few years, with ever-increasing commercial and financial pressures, the fans are still as fervent and dedicated as ever, and still as demanding of the club's motto, *Nil satis nisi optimum* – 'Nothing but the best is good enough'.

David Paul
Liverpool, May 1999.

CHAPTER 1

This is Goodison

Evelyn Truesdale with her sons admiring the Goodison 'silverware'.

Give it to Dixie

My granddad was a season ticket holder at Everton. In fact, he was well over sixty when he eventually gave up going to games on a regular basis. He sat in the Bullens Road stand for years and years. But, in all of those years, my nan had never ever been to a game with him, although she'd always promised to go. So, when the 1966 World Cup was being played in England, one of the match venues was Goodison. Nan went to watch one of the games when Portugal was playing. Both Nan and Granddad said that the atmosphere was absolutely electric. There was roaring and shouting, and a mass of people generally enjoying themselves. Even then, Nan couldn't understand what all the fuss was about. In a quiet moment of the game when there wasn't that much shouting from the stands, Nan stood up, and, just for the hell of it, shouted at the top of her voice 'Give it to Dixie'. Poor Granddad didn't know where to hide. What an embarrassment! She never went to another game.

Karon Meehan

Achieving A Childhood Ambition

I've got photographs from 1987 when we went to Goodison with a relative. He was a good friend of Gordon Watson who's been at Everton since the days of Dixie Dean. In fact, Gordon Watson actually played with the great Dixie Dean, and they carried on their friendship after their playing days were over. At the time, Everton were the holders of the League Championship,

which was the last year that the *Today* newspaper sponsored it. Kendall also had the Manager of the Year trophy, which he'd won the season before. We also held the Charity Shield. When we called into the main reception in Goodison Road, Gordon Watson said, 'Would you like to see the trophies?' I had my three sons with me at the time, who were thirteen, eleven and eight respectively. So all the trophies were taken out of their cases and left in the foyer for us to examine. It was amazing – anyone could have walked off with them! We took loads of photographs whilst we were surrounded by the trophies. He then gave us a personalized tour of Goodison Park – in 1987 that was unheard of! Anywhere behind the scenes was not accessible to the public, but we went all around the trophy room. We then went into the main boardroom. The only place where we were not given access to was the players' changing rooms and this was because there was a training session that day, and the players were due back at any minute. Some of the shots which I managed to take in the Trophy Room would not be allowed today – they're very rare photographs. The whole experience was a lifetime's dream for me, as I'd been watching Everton since the early 1960s. Funny, but through my sons, I actually achieved a childhood ambition.

Colin Truesdale

A Year's Free Fuel

I can go back over sixty-five years. When I first started watching them, I

Proud fans displaying some of the silver gained in the 1984/85 campaign.

was about eight or nine years of age – but that's all a bit hazy now. Before what was known as the 'new' stand was built, it was just a row of houses. There was a back entry to the houses, like so many in Liverpool at that time. I used to go to the game on a bike, like many others at that time. My elder brother would be cycling and I would be sitting on the crossbar. The back entries were used as bicycle storage on match days. We were charged twopence to leave our bikes down the entries, and then it was another fourpence to go into the Boys' Pen. It always annoyed me that the lads who lived there could then just go up to their bedrooms and watch the match from their bedroom windows.

Eventually, the Everton club bought all of the houses on the road, and they were demolished to make way for the new stand – the Bullens Road Stand. The people from the houses were then rehoused and given a year's free fuel. I think that this was because Mr Martindale, a local coal merchant, was a main board director at the time. There was one obtuse character who refused to leave his house. He held out for about two years. We used to go around and watch this character. It was rumoured that he was a Liverpudlian, whilst others said that he belonged to some obscure political party – but nobody ever found out the truth of the matter. When he was eventually evicted, the

Evening Express ran the story, 'Will he get the year's coal?' Again, nobody ever found out whether or not he got the fuel.

John McGovern

A Shilling Deposit on Cups

The very first time I went to a football ground was very strange. I'd never been interested in football, and then John Moores said to me one morning, 'I'm taking Everton over. Make yourself free tomorrow, and come up to the ground with me'. So I went up to the ground to look at the catering facilities, and in those days they were getting in 60-70,000 crowds at every game – that was in 1965, just before the World Cup. I couldn't believe what I saw. They only had a couple of shacks, and they were charging a shilling deposit on cups if you wanted a drink of tea. They had no sinks, but washed glasses and cups in a bucket of water which was kept under the counter. The following day he asked me to go and see him in his private office. He asked me what I thought of the situation, to which I replied that there was a fortune to be made in catering around the ground, providing that the facilities were improved. The shacks were just not selling anything. His reply was 'Get in and get it!' I just couldn't believe it: I was doing enough anyway without taking on a huge increased workload. After the first year of operation, I told him that I needed to build at least fourteen canteens around the ground. He said that I could go ahead, but that any profit which I made must be ploughed back – he just wouldn't release any money! He wouldn't even build a new stadium, even though he'd invested a lot of time in looking around for a suitable site. One day he took me down town, just opposite to the Albert Dock where there was a vacant plot of land where the police station now stands. It was a huge area, and he was thinking of building a new stadium there, but he wouldn't part with any money unless he could see a good profit margin in it.

Ken Davies

Kevin Sheedy with a young mascot. The home game was against West Ham.

Looking towards Gwladys Street from the Director's Box, 1987.

We'll Get You Back Safe

The first game I was ever taken to was in the early Sixties. It happened to be a reserve game. I think that we were playing a team such as Colchester Reserves, and for some reason it was an important game. It was something like they would win the Reserve League if they won this particular game. Everton won 4-0, and at the end of the game just about everybody ran onto the pitch. I was only six at the time, but I can remember running on to the pitch and immediately getting separated from my uncle. As I stood there, I just couldn't believe that I'd actually stopped right on the centre circle where they kicked off from at the start of the game. So there I was, six years old, on the centre of the pitch at Goodison Park, savouring the moment, but with my lower lip quivering because I was lost. Suddenly, a nice policeman picked me up under his arm and said, 'Don't worry lad, we'll get you back safe'.

Nick Hawkins

Six and Six into Gwladys Street

Back in the early Sixties when I first started going to watch Everton things were very different. As children we couldn't afford to go to a football match in those days. We used to go with our mates and wait for three-quarter time. We were then allowed in for nothing and watched what was very often the most exciting part of the game – there was always a lot of action in those days. It was good open football

13

A Ground season ticket for 1969/70 – we won the League that year!

during the 1960s. Later on, when things got a bit better, we could afford a shilling to go into the Boys' Pen, and I think that it was the same over at Anfield – the lads used to go in the Boys' Pen and we used to bunk over into the Gwladys Street at Goodison, but they did the same thing at the Kop. Looking back now, it just wouldn't happen like it did then. People in the ground would actually help us to climb over, and into a more advantageous position. If anyone tried it now, they'd probably be shoved back. We used to pay a shilling to get in, but it was 3s 6d to get into Gwladys Street. When I could afford to go on a regular basis, towards the end of the 1960s, I was paying something like 4s to get into the ground. It was 6s 6d to go into the Gwladys Street stand, and I can

remember thinking that the people who went in there must have been really well off. On one occasion my brother-in-law, who was a good friend of some of the Everton players, got some tickets for one of the derby matches, and he invited me to go along with him. The tickets were for the stands and, as we were queuing up, some of my mates from school came along and couldn't believe that I was in the queue for the stands. They even demanded to be shown the ticket, just to check that everything was 'above board'. The sad fact is that, when we got in there, it was an absolutely terrible view. Unless the ball was directly in line with the goal, then it wasn't worth trying to see any of the game. For most of the time everybody was stood up anyway. I certainly wouldn't have paid six and six for that ticket! To make matters worse, the seats were wooden, so it was better to stand up anyway!

Colin Truesdale

The Boys in All Saints School

I went to a Catholic school, and in those days there was a keen religious division between the Liverpool and Everton football teams, so school was undoubtedly the main influence on me at that time. Most of the other boys in All Saints School were also Evertonians, so it seemed quite natural for me too to become an Evertonian.

Down the road there was Anfield Road School, which was Protestant and most of the boys that we knew at that school tended to support Liverpool. Bear in mind, I'm taking about shortly after the war – maybe round about 1948. In those days Sagar and Lawton were my favourites. It was such a marvellous club with such a marvellous team. To us, as youngsters, it was awe-inspiring to go and watch these players and this team.

Charlie Birch

An Under-Soil Heated Pitch

Everton always had their own private training ground – unlike many other

The legendary Bill Lyken, who was one of the founding members of the Everton Supporters' Club when it was formed in 1958.

15

First Division clubs who would have to use local parks. There's one thing about Everton, they were always streets ahead in terms of innovation. Even before the Second World War they had an under-soil heated pitch. That was well before its time. The only other club that I can think of that had heating under the pitch was Arsenal. Under-soil heating is now relatively common, but it wasn't in those days.

Harold S. Scott

I Wasn't Used to the Cold

When I first came over to England, James, my future brother-in-law, took me to a game. Everton were playing Tottenham at home, and I thought that it was going to be a great game – James said that it certainly looked it on paper. I thought that there'd be goals all the way – in fact, just the sort of game that you would want to see for your first game in England. We got tickets for the Gwladys Street stand, and we were all set for a good afternoon. Unfortunately, and even James agrees, it was one of the most boring games of football that I've ever seen. To make matters worse it was very cold that afternoon, and I wasn't used to the cold. I tried to keep interested by thinking that the game could only get better. About halfway though the second half, I dozed off. Rather than ruin my sleep, James left me to enjoy my afternoon!

Vincenzo Testaverde (Palermo, Sicily)

Missing My Team

At one point when I was in my thirties, I'd been living and working in Berlin for a while. I got round to thinking that the thing which I missed most about Liverpool was the match on a Saturday – there was nothing quite like it in Germany. Even though there were football games, they just didn't seem to have the same atmosphere that was evident at Goodison. So, one Tuesday morning, I decided that I was coming back for the match on the Saturday. I had enough money to get myself to Düsseldorf but no further, so I hitched from Düsseldorf to Calais. I managed, by means which I'm not going to discuss, to get across on the ferry. Arriving in England on the Saturday morning, it then took me two days to get a lift as far as Liverpool. I missed the match, and I've been stuck here ever since!

Paul Lucas

He Didn't Have a Chauffeur Then

When we used to wait for three-quarter time, the gates would open, and we'd stand in the enclosure in Goodison Road. As kids, we would run in and get a good spec for the last twenty minutes or so. John Moores used to park his car in the road directly opposite. He didn't have a chauffeur then, but used to drive himself. He did, however, have his own personalized registration, JM1, even at that time, when personalized number plates hadn't even been heard of by most people. There was never a significant police

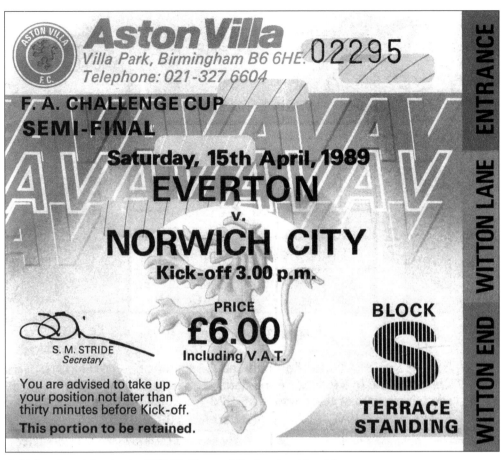

A £6 Standing ticket for the 1989 FA Cup semi-final against Norwich.

presence then. His car was just left at the top of the road without any bother. That brought home the fact that there was warmth in football in those days. There wasn't the need for all the high security that there is today. Kids could go to the match without any fear of trouble or anything of that kind.

Colin Truesdale

His First Game at Goodison

I was asked to look after my two-week-old grandson while my daughter and her husband went out for the night. I said that I would, but I also told my daughter that I'd be going along to the match that night. I wrapped the baby well and went off to the match. I was so excited during the game that one of the policewomen came over and said that she'd look after the baby for me. The next day, when I went to my daughter's, I told my son-in-law that the baby had been christened – he'd been to see his first game at Goodison. My son-in-law went mad, as he's a strong Liverpudlian!

Brenda Clintworth

An Australian baby who's born to be a Blue!

'The Walrus'

There used to be a police inspector who went to both the Everton and Liverpool matches. He was called 'The Walrus'. He was a tall man, about 6ft 7in, he was like a beanpole, but he was in complete control of the situation. He had a big long white moustache which drooped like a walrus – hence his nickname. But make no mistake, he was a disciplinarian, and he didn't let anything get out of hand. I'd love to know if he was still around, as he must have retired a good twenty years ago. He was a character around the ground. These days they have different inspectors for different part of the ground, but his brief was to control the whole of the ground. It just shows how much things have changed.

Colin Truesdale

Temperance Societies Resisted

I asked John Moores if we could sell beer on the ground, because Goodison Avenue became so congested on match days. There were a couple of pubs there, and everyone stayed in them until they were kicked out at three o'clock, and then there was a mad scramble to try and get into the ground before kick-off. I applied for a licence, after going to see the police and explaining my thinking to them. They supported me, but one or two temperance societies put up some resistance. The upshot was that the licence was granted, but I wasn't allowed to serve the beer in glasses. But I had everything worked out. I knew an American/Canadian firm called Lilly Cups and they made paper cups. So I served the beer in paper cups. We only served two types of beer at the time – served directly from the barrels. A beaker of beer retailed for a shilling. We couldn't sell by measure, as the cups could be squeezed whilst the beer was being poured in. Another time a big brewery wanted to build a big glass tank, fill it with beer, and have it sited on top of the Goodison Avenue stand. The beer would then be distributed throughout the ground, but I wouldn't agree to that particular idea. There were too many hazards, we stayed with the good old-fashioned barrels!

Ken Davies

The 'Blonde Biddies'

There were two women that we christened the 'blonde biddies'. They used to stand in the Paddock just by the wall, never arriving later than two o'clock – even if it was going to be a game where there were only likely to be about 20,000 people. Once in position, and with great elaboration, they would get their flasks out and pour themselves a cup of tea, and then maybe have a biscuit. They always had different kinds of biscuits, and they'd pass a few along, so, if we were ever near to them, we always got given chocolate digestives. But, as the game kicked off, out would come the knitting. They would then spend the whole of the game knitting scarves or woollies or socks. Whenever there was an Everton attack, they were totally oblivious, but they would cheer like mad when the gaols went in, even if they looked up and just missed it.

Nick Hawkins

Storage and Distribution Depot

Although completed, the new Bullens Road Stand was never opened before the war. I'm told that the Ministry of Food used it as a storage and distribution depot. It was only opened after the war, in about 1946 I think.

John McGovern

It Just Wasn't Long Enough

I stopped selling draught at the ground and went over to bottled beer. We were then carrying a range of five different beers. We had almost a hundred staff just looking after peoples' needs – we had seventeen canteens around the ground. On one cup-tie, I remember stacking in one corridor over 1,700 bottles of beer, and we were sold out before ten to three in that one canteen! We used to sell, on average, over three thousand meat pies during every match. I then went into sandwiches and filled rolls – I even experimented doing hot dogs. It was very much a novelty at the time. I used the ice-cream trays, which were held around the neck. Underneath the trays we had a Calor gas heater fitted which ensured that the hot dogs were piping hot when they were served. These were made in the workshops at Littlewoods. We just couldn't cope with demand. I wanted to reach the people who never left their seats during any game – more than fifty per cent in a normal game, but, as I say, we just couldn't cope with demand. The ten-minute break at half time just wasn't long enough for them to refill the trays once they'd sold the first batch. We tried to get the interval changed to fifteen minutes but the FA just weren't interested at the time – they didn't even pay us the courtesy of replying to our suggestion.

Ken Davies

ARSENAL FOOTBALL CLUB LIMITED

SOUTHAMPTON V EVERTON
FA CUP SEMI-FINAL
SAT 14 APR 1984 - K.O.   3:00

WEST LOWER TIER

BLOCK	ROW	SEAT	PRI
P	R	62	£6.

atch & Ticket Information 01-359 0131   TO BE RETAIN

Another famous victory at Highbury. Everton beat Southampton 1-0 in the 1984 FA Cup semi-final.

Alphabetical Scores

I've got a memory of these two blokes carrying a billboard around the pitch at half-time. They'd come out as soon as the players went in, and all the billboard promoted was the Everton golden goal. This was what they did at half time. Before the game they had another job, which was to put the corner posts out. It was always the same two blokes every week, wind, rain, hail or snow – they'd be there! At most football grounds in those days there were the letters of the alphabet placed along each side of the pitch. The half time scores were then shown against the various letters. Unfortunately, the scores weren't put up until about twenty minutes into the second half, so, whilst people were checking the scores against

the letters noted in their programmes they would be missing half of the game. If Liverpool were getting beaten then a big cheer would go up as soon as the score was put up. There was no Radio Merseyside in those days!

Colin Truesdale

£2 to Get into the Street End

One day, when our Ross was about three or four, I thought that I would spend a little 'quality time' with him. It was a nice crisp winter's morning and I walked down Stanley Road. We were throwing sticks for the dog, and Liverpool were playing Tottenham at home that day, Everton were away. The game kicked off and we could hear the roar of the crowd. Ross asked what the noise was, but I told him that he didn't really want to know! But then I thought, being open-minded, that I should tell him – knowing full well that he was going to grow up being an Evertonian. As with lots of other families in Liverpool, we're split right down the middle. Sue, my wife, and Kelly, my daughter, are both Liverpudlians, but Ross and me are strong Evertonians. That's just the way it is in Liverpool, and I suppose it will always be like that. To balance things up, the next weekend, when Everton were playing at home, I took him along to Goodison. I think that it was about £2 to get into the Street end then, so we both went in. I also remember buying him an Everton scarf. Ross was sat on my shoulders, so I got in and only had to pay for myself. For years he came

to the match with me. By half-time he was always asleep sat on my shoulders, but this was only after he'd had a cup of tea and an Eccles cake. Funnily enough, he still goes to the game now and has his Eccles cake and cup of tea.

Bob Williams

'Put Him out of his Misery'

I went to the game for years and years with my older brother Tony – we're great mates. Whenever I was feeling flush, I'd mix some G & T into a hip flask, so that we could enjoy a well-earned drink at half time. One Saturday afternoon I was spotted drinking from my hip flask by one of our friendly officers in blue. He immediately cautioned me, stating that I could be

The Charity Shield being savoured by fans in the Winslow – now home of the Supporters' Club.

Lynsey as toffee lady in 1994.

banned from the game for life if I was arrested. One of the wags in the crowd shouted out for everyone to hear, 'Go on, do him a favour, arrest him and put him out of his misery!'

Vinny Riley

I was so Proud of Her

Lynsey Phippard, my granddaughter, goes to every single game that Everton play, both home and away. She knows all the players – she is just like me when I was her age. The first time she was Toffee Lady I just stood there crying, I was so proud of her.

Brenda Clintworth

I Learnt a Lot of New Words

The second match that I went to see was when Everton played against Middlesbrough. They got beat 2-1, so for ninety minutes I learnt a lot of new words in English – mainly swear words I think.

Vincenzo Testaverde (Palermo, Sicily)

The Family Enclosure

I bought a season ticket in 1975 and it cost me £8 – and remember, that's for the whole of the season. I took my son with me, he was only fourteen months old at the time. It was another ten years before he went to another game. This time he understood a little more about what was going on. By the early 1970s

Colin Truesdale and his boys visit the Director's Box at Goodison.

football was becoming a little more commercialized and I decided to give up my ticket. Everton had a player called Asa Hartford. He was a good player, he'd gone from Manchester City to Nottingham Forest. Whilst at Forest, it was revealed that there was a problem with some sort of heart murmur, and they decided to sell him on to Everton. About eighteen months later he decided that he wanted to return to Manchester City, so he sold himself to a newspaper. I remember thinking that if that was the way in which football was moving, then they would have to do without my support. I gave my season ticket away to my nephew, even though there were eight home games left in the season. I started to go again in 1984 when my eldest son began to show some interest

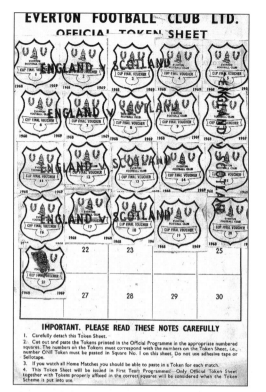

EVERTON FOOTBALL CLUB LTD.
OFFICIAL TOKEN SHEET

IMPORTANT. PLEASE READ THESE NOTES CAREFULLY

1. Carefully detach this Token Sheet.
2. Cut out and paste the Tokens printed in the Official Programme in the appropriate numbered squares. The numbers on the Tokens must correspond with the numbers on the Token Sheet, i.e., number ONE Token must be pasted in Square No. 1 on this sheet. Do not use adhesive tape or Sellotape.
3. If you watch all Home Matches you should be able to paste in a Token for each match.
4. This Token Sheet will be issued in First Team Programmes. Only Official Token Sheet together with Tokens properly affixed in the correct squares will be considered when the Token Scheme is put into use.

Official token sheet for the 1968/69 season.

in football. Just about the same time, Everton started the Family Club. They converted the old Goodison Road Enclosure into the Family Enclosure. There was a £5 initial membership fee for the family, then it was an additional 50p for each child. It was now possible for me to go along to the games with my two sons for a total of £7 if we went in the adverse weather seats.

Colin Truesdale

He Was a Thorough Evertonian

Before he became manager of Everton, Joe Royle was being linked with the Newcastle job, or even the England job. When Joe was manager of Oldham Athletic, one of my friends was a player at Oldham. To cut a long story short, I happened to be on the team coach when they were returning from an away match which they had won 5-0. Joe came and sat next to me because he'd been told that I supported Everton. After we'd shared a few beers, I plucked up the courage to ask him about what he intended to do. You must remember that, when I was a kid, Joe Royle was next to God, along with Fred Pickering. I thought that he probably would be going to Newcastle, but he said that he was waiting for 'the big one'. By this, I thought that he meant the England job, but he soon clarified his answer, and said that Everton was the big one as far as he was concerned. It was the only club that he really wanted to manage. He was a thorough Evertonian – a brilliant man, and I loved him for it!

John Kelly

One-Legged Derek

You would always see lots of characters in the ground. One guy I remember in particular: he was called 'One-legged Derek', a bloke who used to swing in on his crutches, and hop down the steps with the nimbleness of a gazelle on the African plains, and he didn't let the fact that he only had one leg inhibit him in any way. In fact, if anyone in the team was having a stinker, he always used to shout, 'I've only got one leg, and I can do better than that'.

Nick Hawkins

Programmes Were a Penny Each

I was selling programmes at Everton when I was a schoolboy, which was in the Forties – I'm sixty-seven now. When I first started during the war, programmes were a penny each, and we used to get a tanner for every two dozen that we sold, but the main attraction was that you used to get into the match free. Of course, during the war the teams didn't have their usual players on the field, instead they relied on a series of guest players. For instance, if a well-known footballer was stationed at an army camp up at Formby, Everton or Liverpool would be bussing them down to play for them on a Saturday. Anyone in the armed forces always seemed to be well off. They'd often buy programmes, give us a tanner, and let us keep the change. We were able to see top class players and top class goals week in and week out. Everton used to win 8-0, 9-2, 7-1. When the war finished and the League programme started again, they started to charge a little more for entrance and also for the programmes – our wages also went up. Everton had won the League in 1939, and now we were talking about the time when the players were all six years older, but the football in that first season after the war was absolutely magnificent. Football really took off after the war, and we used to enjoy huge gates.

Jim King

Margaret Connor – a devoted fan who had to leave her husband's funeral early because there was a home match that night.

No. 4 — August, 1985

THE
EVERTONIAN

OFFICIAL NEWSLETTER OF THE EVERTON F.C.
SUPPORTERS' CLUB

TROPHIES HERE
TROPHIES THERE . . .

Club members Eddie O'Donovan (left) and Bill Cowan pictured at the Supporters Club with "our" three trophies with Howard Kendall looking on approvingly.

The Evertonian, August 1985.

The Crowds Weren't Segregated

I didn't watch Everton for a long time, but I go and watch them again now. One incident that I vividly remember was in the Sixties when the crowds weren't segregated. We happened to be playing against Sheffield United – they'd just come up from what was the Second Division, and it was the first time that I ever saw any hooliganism as regards fighting. What I actually saw was, as we were leaving about five minutes before the end of the game, some young lads came along, they were obviously very irate for some reason best known to themselves, and they were intent on attacking Sheffield United supporters. It was the first time that I'd ever witnessed anything like that in football. Because of that incident, I didn't go to any football matches for a long time, instead I started to play myself, and that stopped me from going to matches anyway. I then moved away from Liverpool, and I only came back in 1994. Since then I've had a season ticket, and I go along with my kids. Unfortunately, my eldest son is a Liverpool supporter!

Leo Skeete

Plenty of Quality Players

We were banned from Europe after the game at Heysel, and that, in my view, signalled the start of the demise of Everton, even though we had a brilliant team – we'd won the League and we were going places. There were plenty of quality players wanting to join the club at that time: Gary Lineker, Trevor Steven and Gary Stevens – to name just a few. Once we'd been banned from entering Europe, through no fault of our own, I thought that the team began to fall apart. Obviously many of the players wanted to pursue careers that would enable them to win other honours – indeed, many of them did. One of the players that I admire most for being a really true Everton player is Derek Mountfield, he was a fantastic centre half and a great character – he could also score goals. People like him reached out, and could have gone further and further – he was one of the all-time 'greats', but the players that we have now, well…

Lawrence Santangeli

CHAPTER 2

Travelling

Everton supporters enjoying a quiet drink after the game.

Ever Lost a Pair of Tickets?

When I was at university, my granddad would get me a ticket to go to the match with him, and one time he was lucky enough to get a pair of derby tickets for us. I was made up. I got the train home back to Liverpool and met Granddad in town, and we went off to the Shakespeare pub to have a few scoops before making our way to the ground. On the way we stopped off at the Anfield, of all pubs, and had a few more in there. We'd had a few by then, so we started to peg it down to the ground, as we were in imminent danger of missing the kick-off. Just before we got to the turnstile, Granddad said, 'You've got the tickets, make sure that you've got them ready.' Well, I couldn't find them for the life of me. I searched through every pocket. There was no doubt about it, I'd had them when I left, but I didn't have them now! Panic-stricken, I ran all the way back to the Anfield, in the vain hope that I might have left them there – no such luck. I ran back to the ground, and explained to the man on the turnstile that the tickets had been mislaid, but this pleading was to no avail – they must hear similar stories on every match day. A week later, when I was back at the university, and a little more sober than I'd been that night, I was sorting out some washing. Guess what I found in the back pocket of my jeans – yes, the two tickets for the match. It just shows how much we'd had to drink that night. I wrote to Everton asking for a refund, but they suggested that it was my fault, and therefore couldn't agree to any refund. I suppose that they were quite justified in taking this stance, but it was difficult for a hard-up pensioner, and an equally hard-up student.

Karon Meehan

A Season Ticket Holder for Years

We used to come up on the train from Birmingham every other week. There was one week when we got the train at New Street and we were coming to a Cup game, I think that it was Derby County, and we got just outside of Edge Hill and the train broke down. By the time that we got to Goodison the match had already started. We missed the only goal of the game which was scored by Dave Johnson, and that was the end. But then, that was only one of the games ruined because of British Rail. Another time we were on a train heading for Goodison when the train was diverted, and the same thing happened again. By the time that we got to Goodison, the game was all but over. At the moment we're travelling up by coach, and it seems to be pretty reliable. It picks us up at Birmingham and it isn't long before we're pulling up at Stanley Park. So far, touch wood, we've had no mishaps. I live for Everton. I haven't got the same enthusiasm as I used to have, but I still come every other Saturday to every home game. I've been a season ticket holder for years, and next year I'll be entitled to one of the old age pensioners' tickets.

Joseph Somers

A jubilant supporter on his way to Feijenoord. Fortunately, the Channel was very calm that day.

The Big Bass Drum

Six of us set off for Wembley in an old Allegro, and we took along with us a big bass drum that had also been at the 1966 Cup Final. It belonged to Albie Dempsey's dad. His dad had died not long before the Final, so we were desperate to take the drum along with us – especially as we wanted to walk along Wembley Way with it. Half-way down to Wembley we had a blow-out in the car. As the other lads were changing the wheel, I decided to get the drum out of the back of the car and walk up and down the hard shoulder banging it. There were all kinds of blue coaches going past, and they were all banging on their horns as they saw the drum. The sequel is, about four years ago when I used to play a lot of five-a-side football, I was in the showers one day just

relaxing. We were all talking about football, and one of the other guys happened to comment about one of the most stupid things that he'd ever seen. He said that it was in 1984 when, on the way to Wembley, he'd seen this stupid guy walking up and down the hard shoulder banging away on a big bass drum. I had to tell him that it was me! I enjoyed it – I was that idiot.

Lawrence Santangeli

Hitch-hiking in a Suit!

I've got a few memories of Everton, but I'm not sure about some of the dates. We used to hitch-hike a lot when we were young men. We didn't have that much money and it was also much safer hitch-hiking in those days. We used to hitch-hike everywhere. There was one time when me and two other lads, a lad named Ernie Edwards and Harry Slater, decided to hitch-hike down to Leicester. To be honest we never actually got to the match this day because we didn't get enough lifts, but anyway, we were going along the approach road to the M6 on our way down. We were not far from the Uttoxeter road when this old cement wagon came along and stopped for us. You should have seen it, there was dust and grime all over it, but at least it had stopped. The funny thing about it was that me and Ernie, dressed in our Wrangler jeans and jackets, which were all the go in those days, jumped in the cab alongside the driver. Poor old Harry Slater, who was always immaculately dressed – would you believe it, he was hitch-hiking in a suit! Well anyway, he had to get into the back of the lorry where all the lime dust was. When we got to our destination we got out, and Harry was covered in white lime dust. His good suit looked as though it would need a good cleaning. As I said, because we didn't get enough lifts, we weren't able to go to the game that day. We ended up walking around Trentham Gardens all afternoon. We hitch-hiked back when we'd seen enough of the gardens.

Joe Harrison

No Selling To Evertonians

I went to a Cup match and we got the first train down to Birmingham. We then got the first bus out of town so that we could go for a drink, but we had quite a few kids with us. Anyway, there was me, Vera and Kearny. As we were going into the pub there was a doorman, and he wouldn't let us in with the children. We had to tell him that they were only going to the toilet, so he let us all in. We stayed there for a few hours and had a couple of drinks. Later on, me and Kearny went over to the off-licence but they weren't selling anything to Evertonians. We nipped into the butcher's shop next door and, whilst he got our booze for us, we minded his shop for him! We took the stuff from the off-licence into the match.

Linda Harkin

The Fare to the Match was £74

We were a bit tight for cash at the time, and I was saying to the wife that I'd like to go to Rotterdam. She suggested that I went into the whisky bottle to see how much was in there. When I'd counted all of the cash in the bottle, there was almost £79. The fare from Speke airport, including a ticket to the match, was £74! I had £5 to spend.

John Harrison

It's In Your Blood

I remember going to Sheffield Wednesday with my mate Tommy Doran – he's working in America now – and the travel arrangements had been made by AJ. I don't know his second name, but he always does the arrangements, and we call it AJ Tours. It was near the end of the season and Joe

MANCHESTER CITY FOOTBALL CLUB P.L.C.

Maine Road, Moss Side, Manchester   M14 7WN

THE FOOTBALL LEAGUE
MILK CUP FINAL
Replay

Liverpool v Everton

AT MAINE ROAD, MOSS SIDE, MANCHESTER
WEDNESDAY, 28th MARCH 1984
Kick-off 7-45 p.m.

You are advised to take up your position
45 minutes before the kick-off

BLOCK **R**   ROW **15**   SEAT **12**

J.B. Hayford
Secretary

North Stand £6.00

BE RETAINED (SEE PLAN AND CONDITIONS ON BACK)

A ticket for the replay of the 1984 Milk Cup Final against Liverpool.

Royle was still in charge. We left at nine o'clock in the morning, even though Sheffield's only about an hour and a half away. We left from the Elm House on Breck Road. As we were about to leave Tommy decided that he's had enough of going to away games, and he wasn't going to spend any more money on Everton. My view is that if you're an Evertonian it's in your blood, and you've got to go. Tommy spent the rest of the day in the pub, whilst we

32

went over for the game. We were in Sheffield before eleven o'clock, so we went to a little pub called The Horse and Jockey. The people were very friendly and we had a few drinks on what was a lovely summer's day. Kanchelskis had a really cracking game and scored four goals. We won 5-1 in the end. The guy who was supposed to be marking Kanchelskis got hold of him and turned him around – just to see what he looked like, as he'd only seen the back of his shirt throughout the whole of the game! We phoned Tommy up on a mobile phone, but he'd left the pub in disgust.

James Harrison

The Posh Train

Being my age, my first major recollection is the 1966 Cup Final. My dad, as far as I know, was born in Goodison Road, and to the day he died he carried a picture in his wallet of Dixie Dean carrying the cup in the 1933 Cup Final. When we reached the Cup Final, we decided that we were going to go, so we treated ourselves to the posh train with breakfast going down and a meal coming back. I remember that it was a hot day, because I had my mac on. It was an absolute disaster when we were 2-0 down, but the rest of it is history. When that third goal went in for us, my own recollections are just running up and down the terraces of

Joe Harrison with his brother Tommy and Ernie Edwards on their way to Wembley – Joe loves his Guinness!

Wembley like a demented idiot. When we came back to Liverpool, it was like as though we'd just come back from winning the war, basically: there were huge crowds at the station, and all the way home. That was before the glory years of either club really, it was more about the city of Liverpool, it was right at the beginning. None of us could believe the reception we received, it was just like returning as a conquering army coming into Lime Street. It was the same when the Cup itself got back to St George's Hall, it was absolutely incredible.

Malcolm Hadwin

He Hasn't Spoken To Him Since

It was in 1984 when Everton were in the FA Cup Final. Up until that time, I'd never seen Everton win anything. We ended up getting a lift down to Wembley – me and my brother were in one of my mate's cars together with a few of his friends. We got to the Cup Final – cracking day, loads of ale. After the game, which we of course won, we all went to the pub. There was some discussion as to what we should do – should we drive up to Liverpool and celebrate there, or should we stay down in London and have a night on the tiles? We decided that we'd drive back to Liverpool and savour our victory with our mates up there. When we got as far as the M6 a little red light started flashing on the dashboard. Tommy asked his brother Paul, who happened to be driving, whether or not he'd checked the car before they left for Wembley. Before he could give a

satisfactory answer, the car conked out. After waiting for what seemed a lifetime, we were eventually towed to one of the service stations. A local garage then came out to see what they could do, but we were told that they couldn't even begin to look at a repair until the next morning. Tommy and Paul started arguing. The last thing that I remember was Tommy armed with a crook lock, chasing after his brother and making all kinds of unprintable threats. From that day to this he hasn't spoken to him.

Dave Alderton

The Taxi's Exhaust was Falling Off

Although we lost against Liverpool in the Final, I stayed behind to clap the team off the pitch, but when I came out the coach was nowhere to be seen. I looked all over the place, and then, in desperation, I stood at the exit to the car park, hoping that I might just see it, or they might just see me – but no such luck. Loads of coaches went past, but not the one I should have been on. To make matters worse, I'd left my coat on the coach with all my money and cards in. I was determined to get back to Liverpool that night so that I could go to the party that had been arranged at the Everton Supporters' Club. The last coach to come out of the car park was an old charabanc. I flagged him down and told him my predicament. He let me onto the coach, even knowing that I had no money. It was frustrating going up the motorway. All of these fast executive type coaches were flying past us, and there we were

Blue barm cakes outside Wembley.

doing a steady fifty in the middle lane. We stopped at just about every service station on the way up. At half past ten we had still only got as far as the service station at Knutsford. I jumped off the coach at the Jolly Miller and flagged down a taxi. I couldn't believe what happened next. We crawled along at twenty miles per hour to the supporters' club – the taxi's exhaust was falling off! My wife was still waiting for me at the club. She'd been wondering what had happened to me – what a story I had to tell!

Bob Maylor

I Hit Him With My Shoe

When we went to Rotterdam, I had a camera and we'd been around having a few drinks, and we met up with a few of the players that we knew, including Duncan McKenzie. We were all having a good time – until the pub closed that is! We went to find an 'out door' so that we could get some more supplies in. After we'd bought some lager and a bottle of brandy, we met with some of my family who had travelled over with a different company. We were sat in the square, and then we started to play football with the local police. I left my camera on the table whilst I went to the loo, and asked one of the lads to look after it for me. When I got back the camera wasn't there. Later on, in another café, I saw three lads sitting quite nearby, and one of them appeared to have my camera. I went over and asked them about the camera, but they weren't having any, and the next minute this chap hit me. There was a fight, but I didn't get my camera back. I even hit one of them with my shoe! Much later on we met a few more guys, and they said that we should report it to the police, but I just wanted to see the match. By this time I was so flustered that I actually left my bag in another café, but fortunately it was still there when I went back. After the match we went straight on to Wembley, and, when we were in Wembley Way, we met one of the guys who'd been in the fight just a few days before. He was the one that I'd hit with my shoe, and he was now sporting a prize 'shiner'. As it happens he'd been an innocent bystander the other day. But, he'd actually done something about it, and now presented me with my camera. He also gave me a bottle of brandy!

Brenda Clintworth

Pouring Down Throughout

The '86/87 season when we won the League stands out in my mind. I remember going to an away game at Arsenal. I went down with Paul and Laurence on the train, I was about sixteen or seventeen at the time. I'd just started work and I was getting a bit of money in my pockets. I wasn't getting that much, so Dad paid for my season ticket, but I funded all the away games myself. We went down in a really old train – I swear that it took us almost three hours to get as far as Crewe. Arsenal had an open end at the time, and it was absolutely pouring down throughout the game. I was soaked through. It was cold and damp, but we went ahead – it was great. There was better news to come – Wimbledon were

beating Liverpool 2-1 at Anfield. Those games were both vital in the run-up to the championship.

James Harrison

Not a Good Reception

We organized a coach trip up to Oldham for a cup game. When we got back on the coach after the match two of our lads had been arrested – so, as we'd all gone together, we decided that we were all coming back together. We went 'mob-handed' around to the police station where we didn't get too good a reception! A few more guys from our group got arrested in the police car park, and our coach was then escorted back to the motorway. As soon as we got back to Liverpool we jumped in a taxi and went all the way back to Oldham. The police got quite a surprise as we walked in. We explained that we needed our mates back. Before too long we could hear Everton songs being sung in one of the cells. Our mates were soon escorted out, with coppers flanking them on both sides. One of the policemen asked what had happened to the famous Scouse humour. By this time, one of the lads had a couple of broken fingers and his nose was wrapped half-way around his face – all he said was, 'How do you expect me to have a sense of humour when you've broken my last ciggy?'

Dave Kelly

I Fell Asleep in the Second Half

When we went to Amsterdam last August we went down by car. I drove down to Harwich with a few of my mates, and we got the boat across to the Hook of Holland. When we got to Amsterdam, it just happened to be the Gay Sports Weekend, so we couldn't get a room anywhere. We walked around looking for some time, and then this little man approached us and said that he could get us a room. We all drove down in a taxi as far as this tenement building. But, as the room looked OK, we decided to stay there for the night. The next day we caught the train down the line to where the match was due to be played. The match wasn't that exciting. In fact, I fell asleep in the second half. We lost 2-0. When we left the stadium everything appeared to be dead in the middle of this little town. We wandered around for some time until we found the main square which was full of Evertonians. There was a great atmosphere, with some of the lads playing football with the locals. We had a great night after that.

Paul Durose

Alternative Arrangements

One of the funniest things that I've ever seen, was when we were going down the motorway to Wembley. It was a lovely sunny day, when, all of a sudden, the lad who was driving, Albie Dempsey, put on the windscreen wipers. We wondered what the hell he was doing – we soon found out. In front of us there was a single decker corpy bus from Liverpool, and there was a spray of liquid coming from it. As we pulled alongside the bus, we saw a queue of men lined up in the coach. The front door of the bus had been jammed open with a handy traffic cone, and they were taking turns to pee out of the door. This was because there were no facilities on the bus! There were lots of executive coaches on the road that day, and they obviously had all of the facilities on-board, but this little corpy bus couldn't run to that, so the lads had to make alternative arrangements.

Lawrence Santangeli

We Climbed Into Molineux

I remember the 1966 season when Everton drew 0-0 with Manchester City at Goodison, and then 0-0 at Maine Road – I think that it was the sixth round of the Cup. We then had to travel down to Wolverhampton for the second replay. It was a mid-week game, so, once again, I hitch-hiked down with Jimmy. We got into a builder's yard, took a ladder, and then climbed into Molineux. We stayed there all day until it was time for the game. We hid in the toilets, and when the gates opened at half six we came out of our hiding place and mingled with the rest of the crowd. We'd only been in the ground about two minutes when Jimmy announced that he needed to go to the toilet!

Joe Harrison

Everton fans lost outside Rotterdam.

Well, it Hit the Fan, didn't it!

Do you remember years ago when *Match of the Day* first came on? Well, my little brother, who's about thirty-six now, he used to tell my parents that he was going fishing on a Saturday morning – at the time he was only fifteen or sixteen years of age. My parents were really pleased with him because he'd got up off his backside and gone and got himself a paper round. He also used to help the local milkman, and they were really pleased that he was doing something active in order to get a few bob for himself. He had all of this fishing kit, and my mum would get up all kinds of hours in the morning and make him loads and loads of sandwiches, and give him bottles of lemonade. She'd make sure that he had all of his gear before he fell out of the

door, with all his fishing rods, and bags and baskets and everything else. It wasn't until about six months later that I was sitting in the front room, it was about nine o'clock, and I was watching telly. He'd come in and gone straight to bed. Anyway, I carried on watching the telly, and the match happened to be Everton playing Chelsea at Stamford Bridge. It wasn't until I saw the action replay that I realised who was standing behind the goal in Stamford Bridge. My little brother, young as he was, would save up his pocket money, and then tell my mum and dad that he was going fishing, and then bugger off to London with his mates on the train. When I saw it, I just couldn't believe it, but when they showed the replay, there was no doubt about it. It was a shot of the goalkeeper at full stretch, and right behind the goal was our Ronnie with his arms in the air. Well, it hit the fan didn't it! My dad shouted, 'Get down these stairs right away!' Ronnie came down all angelic-like, just trying to find out what was the matter. He was asked, 'Where were you today? You weren't at Stamford Bridge were you?' His face just dropped! After that, when the truth was out, he started to buy season tickets – and he's been a season ticket holder ever since.

Bob Williams

2,121 Miles to See Everton Beaten

This is an account of a fantastic journey that I made some years ago. How it all started was when we were due to play Zaragoza in the second round of the European Cup-Winners' Cup – we'd already seen off Aalborg in the first round. There were three of us in the 300 Club who wanted to go along, Allan Brereton, Billy Davies and me. Alan knew Harry Catterick, so he phoned him, only to be told that there were no flights to Zaragoza, as they only had a military airport there. Harry Catterick said that the team was flying out to that airport, so we tried to get on the flight with them. Unfortunately, because of restrictions that the insurance company had imposed, the flight had to be limited to the players and club officials. We were told however, that, if we managed to get there, there would be tickets waiting for us. We decided to drive overland. We left Huyton at 11.30 on the Monday evening and headed for East Leigh

Some of the Harrison family off to Wembley in 1985.

Airport which is near to Southampton. We took the driving in turns – this was before the days of the motorways of course. It was thick fog throughout the night, but we still arrived at East Leigh by 5.30 in the morning. We had a few hours' sleep in the car, and then we left the airport at 9.30 in the morning. We touched down shortly after eleven – French time. Driving through France was very different to say the least. We swapped drivers every hundred miles or so, stopping at Nantes for a meal and a little break. It was November, and there was torrential rain all the way through France. The rain didn't help, as none of us were familiar with French roads or French driving. We eventually arrived at the Spanish border at three thirty on Wednesday morning. We then continued across the Pyrenees – alternating driving throughout. It was really bad weather, and included mist, fog and rain all the way down to Zaragoza. By the time we arrived we were all well and truly knackered. Although we'd taken turns at driving, there wasn't that much rest when you weren't driving. We were tired and damp, and feeling quite sorry for ourselves after our difficult journey. We'd driven almost 1,000 miles since we left home – and it felt like it!

We were booked into the Grand Hotel. This was the only reasonable hotel in town, so it came as no surprise to find that the team was also staying there. The rooms weren't ready, so we decided to go and find Harry Catterick so that we could get our tickets. He was surprised, but delighted, to see us. We slept until about six, and then we went for a meal. By chance we bumped into a Zaragoza player who took us to the ground. He showed us all round the ground and made us feel very welcome. Unfortunately the seating arrangements at the ground left a lot to be desired, but then, you can't have everything can you? Zaragoza won 2-0, and Morrisey was sent off – that didn't help us. Apart from three other fans who had hitch-hiked all the way across from Liverpool, we were the only Everton supporters at the game. After Morrisey was sent off we had our own police guard surrounding us – I don't know just what they thought we were going to do.

We had a few drinks with some of the players before returning to our hotel and having a good night's sleep before the long drive back the next day – a drive which none of us was looking forward to. If we'd have won, then it might have been a different story. We set off after breakfast and then had a little problem with the brakes when we were going over the Pyrenees. When we got to the French border they wouldn't let us out of the country. Remember, it was still in the days of Franco. It was easy getting into the country, but very difficult to get out! They eventually found an interpreter, so we were able to leave shortly after that.

At one o'clock in the morning it was my turn at the driving wheel. The car was a new Vauxhall 101 with less than six thousand miles on the clock. All of a sudden this little red light started flashing on the dashboard. I hadn't got a clue as to what it could be, and immediately thought that there was something wrong with the engine. When I woke up the owner of the car, he informed me that it was the petrol warning light. I'd never come across such a sophisticated device before.

Every car that I'd ever driven up until that time just had a simple gauge. We searched all over the place for a garage, but at one o'clock in the morning in the middle of rural France there's not much chance of finding one! We found ourselves in the centre of a small town, so we decided to siphon some petrol from one or two of the cars which were parked around the square. Unfortunately none of the cars that we tried seemed to have very much petrol in. Then, as we were leaving the town, we found a wrecked car, and, believe it or not, the tank was almost full of petrol. We spent the next half-hour carefully emptying all of the petrol from this wreck into our car.

We finally got to Le Havre airport, but the freighter was already full, so we then had to drive on to Cherbourg where we caught the overnight ferry back to England. We docked early Saturday morning, and then drove as fast as we could back to Liverpool – we were playing a home game that afternoon! After we'd had lunch, we were straight along to Goodison! 2,121 miles to see Everton get beaten!

Charlie Birch

And He Went And Missed It!

I remember going to Oxford, and there were two games left to go in the season, and Lineker from two yards out headed the ball to the ground and it bounced over the bar. Oxford then raced down to the other end and scored. They beat us 1-0. The same night Liverpool won 2-1 at Leicester and then went on to win the League. Travelling back from Oxford that night was like travelling back from Australia. Every mile was a thousand miles. It must have been the best opportunity that Lineker had been presented with all season and he went and missed it!

Bob Maylor

The Longest Route to the Ground

We'd walk to the match every week from Lodge Lane, down Tunnel Road, Durning Road, Hope Road, Sheil

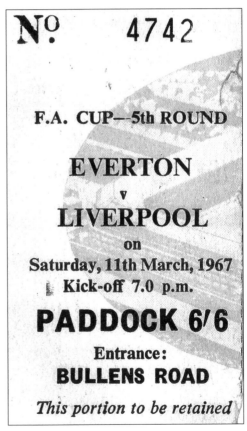

Nº 4742

F.A. CUP—5th ROUND

EVERTON
v
LIVERPOOL
on
Saturday, 11th March, 1967
Kick-off 7.0 p.m.

PADDOCK 6/6

Entrance:
BULLENS ROAD

This portion to be retained

One of our most memorable games, 11 March 1967. We beat Liverpool in the Fifth Round of the FA Cup. Alan Ball scored the one and only goal in the 44th minute.

Everton fans off to the 1985 Final.

Road, Belmont Road, Oakfield Road and as far as Sleepers Hill and down that way. This was one of the longest routes to the ground, but there was a good reason – there were more pubs if we went that way. Dad popped into most of them, and we'd be sheltering in the doorway with a bottle of lemonade which he'd have sent out to us. Funnily enough, when my own family were growing up, and I used to take my lads to the match, I carried on the tradition. I used to take my eldest lad when he was still running for the Liverpool schools team. I took him into the Sandon, which has got a great history as far as football is concerned. Apparently, Everton used to change in there when Anfield was their home ground. The George Mahon Cup, which was played

for on a regular basis, was actually stolen from there. When we went past Anfield, we were always instructed to close our eyes, as we were passing the ground of the opposition.

Stan Cain

Down the Motorway to Wembley

I can't remember what year it was now, but it was one of the Liverpool Cup Finals, it must have been the early Eighties and Liverpool won it. I've got two sons who, at the time, were about ten or twelve. I'd got my tickets so I was going to the match, and they were both green with envy – one supports Everton and one supports Liverpool, as is so often the case in this city. I actually had managed to get three tickets, but I didn't tell the boys anything about this – as far as they knew, Dad had a ticket for the game, and that was that! On the morning of the final we got them up at about six o'clock, and they just couldn't understand why they were being woken up at such an unearthly hour. I told them that we were all going down to the match, but it took quite a while to sink in – well, it would do at that time in the morning, wouldn't it? They got themselves out of bed and dressed, and then it was off down the motorway to Wembley. The atmosphere going down the motorway was great, and, yes, there can be an atmosphere on a motorway – on that day it was absolutely tremendous, you've never seen so many blue and red scarves trailing out of cars. People were banging their horns in recognition, and that was all the way down the M6 and the M1. We were one of the classic cars if you like, we had red scarves trailing out of one side, and blue scarves trailing out of the other.

Malcolm Hadwin

What's Wrong With Your Face?

Everton were playing West Bromwich Albion in the Cup Final in 1968. Most fans travelled by coach in those days, and it took an absolute age to get there. We got beat, which didn't help, but it was a bad game anyway. If it had been a bad game and we'd won, then it

Waiting to go into the Final.

might have been a different story, but in the event we didn't. I didn't get back home until three o'clock in the morning. We'd just moved into a new house in Walton, and my sister-in-law was staying with my wife to keep her company. When I banged on the door at that time, she came down the stairs and opened the door with a very frosty face. The first thing that she said to me was, 'And what's wrong with your face?' She wasn't into football!

Joe Harrison

We Used to Hide under the Tables

Joe, my brother, had his mates and I had mine, but we both used to meet up at the away games. We used to hitch-hike down to the games, just like Joe, but we were better at it than him! We used to hitch-hike there, but then we used to 'bunk' the train back. When we 'bunked' on the train, we used to hide under the tables when the inspectors came around. We used to go to Sunderland and all over the place. In fact, it was whilst we were at Sunderland that we all fell asleep after a memorable night. The postman woke us up on his early rounds the next morning.

John Harrison

We Beat Tottenham 4-1

We played a semi-final against Tottenham and won 4-1. We left at seven o'clock in the morning, and it was a twelve o'clock kick-off. It was the

first semi-final being played that day – United *v.* Crystal Palace was the other one. Anyway, at seven o'clock we were stood outside the Elm House. We were only going as far as Leeds, which isn't a million miles away, so we had a few bottles of Bud before we left. When we got there we went into the Leeds supporters' club. We got there at ten o'clock, and before eleven everything was sold out! All they had left was bottles of shandy and some home-brew wine. The game itself was alright though.

James Harrison

We Got as Far as Potters Bar

Freddie Armstrong always used to organize coaches when we went to away games. The unfortunate thing was the coaches had a habit of breaking down before we got to the match. But, on this occasion, the new executive coaches were just coming in, and Freddie said that he could organize one – but it would cost a little more. Freddie was a real character. He was a big black jovial man, and known to both fans and players. Anyway, we signed up for this trip. We thought that we were going to get our breakfast served on the way to the game, but instead we were served with a few jam butties. The coach did all right until we got as far as Potters Bar, and then it broke down. The scenes were sheer bedlam, with fans flagging down cars and begging a lift to the match, or even offering to pay ridiculous prices just to get there.

Dave Alderton

The Highlight for Me

The night before we went to Rotterdam, we were sat there in the supporters' club – there were about six or seven coaches going. On the way out to the coach we called into the off-licence and bought a full tray of cans. I carried the beer and my mate carried the bags. We were called onto coach number four, but the driver wouldn't let us on with the beer. He insisted that we'd never get through Dover with beer on the bus. That aside, the Rotterdam trip was the highlight for me. We won the cup, came back on the Thursday, and then we were off down to Wembley on the Saturday. Like so many other fans, I still believe that if those games would have been played the other way around, with the FA Cup Final first, then we would have beaten Manchester United that year. The players were just dead on their feet – even the fans couldn't muster that much enthusiasm. We were so full of what had happened in Rotterdam on the Wednesday.

Bob Maylor

'Fazakerley Sidings!'

It was always difficult to get tickets, as we were always hard up in those days. Any cash that we got went on the home. I didn't even have a car at the time, let alone money to get to the game. We managed to get a few tickets for an away game, but we couldn't afford to pay for the journey down. And then we had a brainwave. Do you remember the old Fazakerley sidings? We walked down there with lots of heavy-duty

Young Liam was on the ream coach getting autographs – but his aunt thought that he was lost!

Very weary, on the way home after the 1985 FA Cup Final against Manchester United.

plastic bags, and then we picked scrap iron from the ground. We collected about fifteen bags of scrap iron, but then we had no way of getting to the scrap yard. In the end we got a taxi. At first the cabby wasn't going to take us, but we explained that we had to get to the game on Saturday, and that we didn't have a bean. He relented, stopping first at the weighbridge before carrying on to the yard, Rifkin's in Kirkdale. When we weighed everything in, we came out loaded. We paid off the taxi and we had enough cash left to travel to the game in style, get ourselves a good meal and a few bevvies. On a few occasions after that, whenever we were skint, we'd look at one another and just say 'Fazakerley sidings!'

Bob Williams

Two and Six Return from Ireland

I've been coming up to Goodison since 1958. In the old days we never had a supporters' club, so we had to make our own way by train. This was very expensive. I've supported Everton for years, since the days when I lived in Dublin. They were the first English team to have a supporters' club in Ireland. Glasgow Celtic had one, but they're Scottish. Peter Farrell and Tommy Eglington got transferred from Shamrock Rovers to Everton, and my loyalty went with them. Ever since then I've been an Evertonian. They also bought Jimmy O'Neill and Mick Meagon and Don Donovan. In fact, they had six Irish players in the 1953 Cup semi-final against Bolton Wanderers. That's one of the reasons

46

why they have such a large Irish following. In the old days, it was possible to come across on the boat for two and sixpence. People used to come and watch the great Dixie Dean play – two and six return from Ireland!

Joseph Somers

Straight for the Station

We went down to Plymouth when we'd been drawn against them in the Cup. It was a long journey all the way down from Lime Street. It took us about seven and a half hours to get there. We had a drink before the game and then made our way to the ground. We won 3-0. Coming back we were just about to nip into a boozer, but one of my mates said that there'd be plenty of beer on the train, so we made straight for the station. When we got on the train we found that all they were selling was bottles of insipid shandy! We had a few of them, but it wasn't really the way that we wanted to celebrate on what was to

Ticket for the Merseyside Final of 1986.

be an eight-hour journey home. I suppose that the main thing was that we'd won.

Joe Harrison

He Lived to Tell the Tale

My brother worked away as a printer, but he still came home for matches. One year we were all going down to the Final at Wembley, but we couldn't get any tickets for the coach. John got hold of one of the stubs, and then printed off about forty of them. All of our mates were given one, and he sold the rest in the pub. On the morning of the Final, we made sure that we were on the coach first. A few minutes later the other passengers came along. In the event there must have been about seventy people trying to get onto this thirty-six seater coach! Somehow he lived to tell the tale.

Dave Alderton

Villa is Nowhere Near Dudley

We were going down to a game being played at Aston Villa's ground, but for some unexplained reason, our coach driver decided to take us via Dudley. Aston Villa's ground is nowhere near Dudley, so, after we'd spent ages trying to negotiate our way through the traffic, we decided that we'd had enough. We ditched the coach, went for a few drinks and then got public transport to the ground. We were only a few minutes late arriving. During the time that we were in Dudley,

I'd passed a comment to the effect that I couldn't understand anyone wanting to live or work in such a godforsaken place. I'd just finished my first year at university and I was due to go on a three-month work placement. When I went back to the university on Monday, I had to see my tutor to discuss my placement – guess where I was going – yes, IMI Yorkshire Fittings at Dudley!

James Harrison

We Sat Drinking Irish Whiskey

In 1985 we qualified for the Cup-Winners' Cup, and in the third round we were drawn against University College, Dublin. I went across with one of my mates. We left Liverpool on the Tuesday evening at ten o'clock, and the bar was open until one. We drank Guinness with Paddy's as chasers all night. We arrived in Dublin at about seven o'clock in the morning, but the game wasn't due to be played until half past seven that night. We found somewhere to have our breakfast, and then realized that we had a very long wait until the pubs opened. Just then, this guy tapped us and asked if we wanted to find a good pub. He gave us directions to a little pub, and told us to knock on the door and tell them that Seamus sent them. We found the pub, knocked on the door and were welcomed in with both arms! The place was chock-a-block full of Evertonians – I'd never seen so many! They'd got the early boat over, and had been there since the night before. From that moment on, everything was fine. The game wasn't too memorable, but we'd had a really great time. We drew 0-0, but that wasn't so important at the time. We got back onto the boat and headed straight for the bar. After a few drinks we dozed off. Some little while later we came to, and we could see the harbour lights. I gave my mate a shake, and we headed towards the gangway. One of the crew stopped us and asked where we were going. I said that we wanted to be first off the boat, as I had to get to work that day. He told us that we hadn't left Dublin yet. The boat had actually sailed, but then had to turn back as there was some trouble on board. We sat drinking Irish whiskey until seven o'clock in the morning.

Bob Maylor

John Parrott was Just Behind Me

I went to a semi-final game with a friend of mine. We went down on the coach, and there was a small hall just by the ground. We went in for a cup of tea and some lemonade, as we had the children with us. John Parrott was stood just behind me. I'd always thought that he was a Liverpudlian, but how wrong can you be? At the time, John was playing in the Embassy World championship snooker at the Crucible in Sheffield.

John Harrison

Two of Everton's travelling fans, Godfrey and Alf – they travel all the way from Malta!

A 16s ticket for the Charity Shield game against Chelsea in 1970. Everton won 2-1.

Anything to Watch Everton

In 1963 Everton were playing West Bromwich Albion. It was a mid-week game and we were travelling down by train. One of our mates, Jimmy, couldn't afford the train fare, but I thought that he'd turn up one way or another. Sure enough, just before we were due to leave Lime Street, Jimmy was sat next to us. He'd managed to get through the barrier, and had entered by the door on the other side of the carriage. It was one of the trains with doors on both sides. We used to do anything to get to watch Everton.

Joe Harrison

'And When Did You Come Out?'

It was New Year's Day in the late Seventies or even 1980, and it was snowing, but we always went to the game, wherever it happened to be – it was just one of our traditions. The game was being played at Bolton, and we thought that, because of the snow, it would be called off, but it wasn't. We drove through the blizzards to Bolton, and when we got there it was just the same as Liverpool – about three inches of snow. We went to the working men's club and had a few pints before making our way to the ground. They'd cleared the pitch, and there was snow piled high around the touchlines. We were all stood on the terraces and it was still snowing. We all had two or three inches of snow on our heads and shoulders. Peter Reid was playing for Bolton and George Wood nearly crocked him – it was accidental, and due entirely to the atrocious conditions. It was a farce. At the end of the first forty-five minutes when the score was 1-1 they abandoned the game. The funny thing was, there had been about four lads stood next to us in short sleeved shirts – they must have come straight on to the game from a New Year's Eve party. We were covered in snow, but these four were just stood there as though it was a sunny day. One of our mates asked where their coats were, and they replied by saying that it was sunny when they came out. Quick as a flash, a wag behind shouted, 'And when did you come out – August?'

Ray Anderson

We Got Back the Following Day

When we went to Rotterdam – we'd got the coach journey cheap from the Polytechnic, as my wife was a student there – we got a coach organized, but there were that many who wanted to go, that we had to sort out a few more. On the way down to the Channel, one of the coaches broke down – in fact, it broke down a few times. We eventually arrived at Dover and managed to get across, but we were running very late. Believe it or not, on the way back, exactly the same thing happened. We didn't arrive back in Liverpool until late the following day – some fifteen hours after we were due back!

Paul Durose

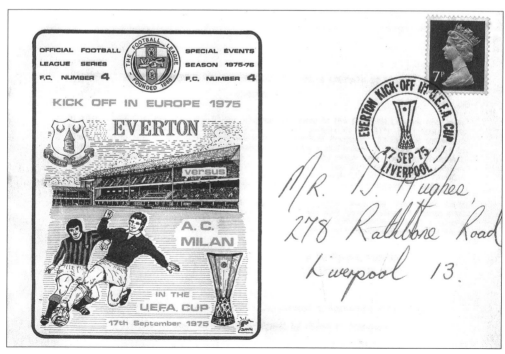

Commemorative programme cover for the Everton v AC Milan UEFA Cup Final in 1975.

CHAPTER 3

Cup Games

1966 Final programme – Everton *v.* Sheffield Wednesday.

Robin Hood

I travelled with my uncle and father to see Everton play away in a cup game at Notts Forest. Leaving aside some appalling refereeing and a less than solid display by Andy Rankin, Everton lost 3-2. The story, however, is about the journey to the ground. Being unfamiliar with the city centre in Nottingham, my uncle spotted a car full of Everton supporters stopped alongside a policeman. Clearly they were asking for directions to the ground. Not wanting to ask the policeman the same question twice, my uncle thought that the simplest solution was to follow the other car. After fifteen minutes of driving in and out of the Saturday traffic in Nottingham, we returned to the same spot and the same policeman. To make sure that he could hear the instructions from the policeman, my uncle pulled up right behind the other car and wound his window down, just in time to hear the driver say 'It's no wonder you lot never caught Robin Hood!'

John Boardman

My First Final

The 1968 Cup Final – I can't remember the last digit of the season ticket number, but mine had failed to be selected in the early rounds of the cup competition and it failed again when the distribution for the Final was announced. There was an angry outburst from fans in the same predicament and the club relented. I got my ticket and off I went to Wembley. As I didn't qualify in 1966 this was my first visit to Wembley to see a final. There is no need to dwell on the outcome of the game, except I still believe that the referee should have had a closer look at the way Williams kept Husband out of the game. My abiding memory of the day is eventually getting back to Liverpool Lime Street a lot later than we had thought. (Nothing changes on the railways!) There wasn't a taxi in sight (or all the Liverpudlian taxi drivers were hiding) so I ended up walking home to Kirkdale. During the course of the walk I and my fellow walkers received advice on every conceivable method of suicide from vocal Liverpool supporters, who had spent their evening toasting the goal scoring genius of the man who is now better remembered for his off-key singing in *Fantasy Football*. When I arrived home I was greeted by my mother with the famous words 'Don't worry, son, there's always next year.' Those were the days when you believed that was true!

Geoff Jones

An Epic Final

I went to Wembley in 1995 with my dad and witnessed an epic final, and then I went to a few European games during the next season. The first European match that I saw was against Reykjavik. We won that game, but we went out in the next round when we were beaten by Feijenoord. I was very disappointed when Joe Royle went, as I didn't think that he'd been given a fair chance. In his first season, they hadn't won a game until November, and then he took them into Europe in the next season. We finished sixth in the league that season, and the next season we were somewhat further down – so they sacked him!

Andrew Skeete (aged 15)

I Felt Extremely Depressed

I remember the Cup Final in 1966, but unfortunately I didn't go to that one as I couldn't get a ticket. I watched the game on television, and felt extremely depressed when we were losing 2-0, and then completely ecstatic when we won. I borrowed a video of that game, and it's amazing how your memory plays tricks on you. A pal of mine who went to the game watched it with me. We both had completely different recollections of the game, but when we watched the video it was different again! We both thought that our first goal was scored much later in the game, but of course it wasn't.

Peter Spear

John Moores Gave me his Wallet

In 1966 I went to Wembley with my brother, but we only had one ticket for the two of us. We went along to the hotel where all the players and directors were staying, hoping to get another ticket, but we were unlucky. As we were leaving I happened to see John Moores and asked him for his autograph. He signed the autograph on a piece of paper that I'd given him, resting the paper on

Outside St George's Hall on the triumphant return, 1966.

54

his wallet whilst he signed. As he gave me back the signature, he also passed me his wallet. Before I realised what had happened he was gone. I went to look for him, eventually found him, and returned his wallet. He was so grateful that he presented me with a free ticket for the game – so we were both able to go!

Brenda Clintworth

Chicken Held out Towards the Sun

Everton were one of the first English teams to play on the Continent. The first trip abroad was to Greece. John Moores who was going along asked me if I would be able to do the catering for the whole of the party, as he wasn't too sure about the reliability of foreign chefs. We managed to get permission from the hotel to use their kitchens, with our staff doing all the cooking. We sorted out all the menus for the time we were going to be over there, as we were going for a few days. We packed up all of the food that we would need for the trip and I had it put into special camping freezers, and then it all went into the plane's cargo hold. While we were on the plane Harry Catterick wasn't feeling too well, so he came along to me and asked if he could have some chicken when we arrived, rather than the fillet steak which everybody else would be having. But, all the chickens were frozen. I got permission from the pilot to go into the cargo hold, and I took out one of the chickens. For the remainder of the flight I sat by the window with the chicken held out towards the sun, so

Brenda at Wembley.

that it would be ready for cooking when we landed – it must have looked quite a sight!

Ken Davies

Temple did it Again!

My favourite game has to be the Final when Trebilcock scored the first two goals and then Derek Temple scored the winner. He got the ball and ran practically the length of the field to score – I'll never forget that goal, and I dare say, neither will many other Everton fans up and down the country. Strange to say, the first game in the following season was a home game and we were playing Sheffield Wednesday. The game was almost a carbon copy of

55

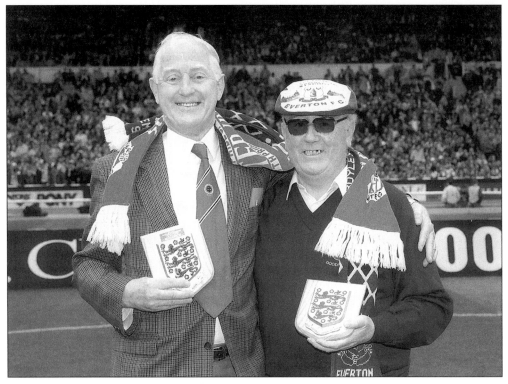

Jim King's proudest moment came at the FA Cup Final in 1995 against Manchester United. The Football Association invited him to go onto the pitch with his opposite number from United and welcome the fans.

the one that I'd watched at Wembley. Temple did the same thing again!

Charlie Birch

Proudest Moment as an Evertonian

I've been secretary of the supporters' club for fifteen years now, but my proudest moment came at the Cup Final in 1995 against Man United. The Football Association invited me to go onto the pitch with my opposite number from United, and we exchanged trophies which had been donated by the Football Association. They were to promote friendship between clubs. We walked to the centre spot, and we both had to make a speech of welcome to the visiting fans – I welcomed United, and he welcomed Everton. It was a particularly good game because we won, and it topped off a particularly fine day. It made me feel really proud to be an Evertonian when I walked off that centre spot and the crowds were all cheering – he was walking towards the United end, and I was walking towards the Everton end. It was absolutely magnificent! Just to feel that I'd represented the blue half of Merseyside was my ambition achieved.

Jim King

A Crowd of over 78,000

I always remember a game against Burnley where there was a crowd of over 78,000. I started off in Gwladys Street, but I finished up watching the game sat behind the net on the running track because the crush was so great. I seem to think that it was a cup game, but I'm not too sure. Even the roads outside of the ground were absolutely crowded.

Malcolm Hadwin

A Piggyback to the Travellers Rest

I went to a replay at Hillsborough with my dad and our Raymond. We walked down to the Leather Bottle, from where the coach was leaving. My dad nipped across the road and got himself half a bottle of scotch. His excuse was that it was a cold day, and it would warm him up – this is on a 'dry' coach by the way. We eventually got to Sheffield and stopped just by a pub called the Travellers Rest – it's not too far from the ground itself. The game was a half past seven kick-off, and we'd arrived there at half past six. Our Raymond and me had stand tickets, but Dad only had a ticket for the ground. I gave him my stand ticket, and then went off to take my place in the ground. I assumed that they'd be leaving as soon as they'd finished their drinks, but I was told afterwards that they didn't leave the pub until almost twenty past seven. After the game I wandered back to the bus, to find everyone waiting to drive back to Liverpool over the Woodhead Pass – everyone that is apart from Raymond and my dad. It was now almost half an hour after the bus should have departed to get back home. The next thing we saw was Raymond giving my dad a

Even in 1971 Gwladys Street regulars always went to the Winslow before going to the match.

Some fans from the supporters' club leaving on their way to Wembley.

piggyback all the way to the bus. Seemingly, they'd made an agreement during the game that every time Everton scored they'd have a sip of whisky. As they only scored once, the rules had to be changed. The new rule was that every time Everton passed the ball, then they'd have a sip of whisky. Because the game went to extra time, the whisky really did take a pounding – and so did my dad!

Steve Bretherton

We Were a Bag of Rags

I'll go back to 1966: I was working in a tannery at the time – doing well and going to night school at Runcorn College of Further Education. Anyway, through the night school, there was a trip out to Bolton to go and look at a tannery. So, on the Friday we were setting off for Bolton, and, as luck would have it, on the Saturday Everton were playing against Manchester United in the semi-final of the FA Cup – it was being played in Bolton. So, me and this other guy that was with me decided to go up to Bolton, do the deed with the tannery, and then just stay overnight. We didn't have any tickets for the match, but we decided to do something about that. We had a bite to eat followed by a few pints and put the word around that we were after tickets. There was a guy who had tickets but he was a little bit cagey with them. We went outside to do the deal. After everything was sorted out, the local lad gave the signal to tell all of his mates that it was a legitimate deal, and that there was no need for the 'heavies'. We were then faced with the problem of having nowhere to sleep. We came across a boarding house and said that we wanted a bed for the night. As we went in there was all sorts of hassle between the husband and wife who owned the boarding house. I didn't want to know any of this, so I said that we'd find somewhere else. We walked until well past midnight, and by this time we were full of ale. We came to a railway signal box, and just down the road from there, there was a workman's hut. It was amazing, there was a bench and a table inside – ideal to spend the night there. The soft lad that I was with went and put the lights on. Everywhere else was pitch black, and this hut lights up all of a sudden just like a beacon. The next thing, the people in the signal box had obviously spotted the light, so we had to get out of there fast. In the end we laid our heads to rest in Marks & Sparks doorway in the centre of Bolton. We were shrivelled up in the corners looking like two waifs and strays. The next thing that I could hear was people walking past going to work – they were wearing clogs – I couldn't believe it! It was still only quarter to five in the morning. They were all looking at me and my mate as they went on their way to work. We were a bag of rags! We sorted ourselves out and then went to find somewhere where we could have a wash and brush-up. After breakfast we met a few Scousers on their way to the semi-final. The rest is history. Charlton, Law and Best were all playing for Man U. but, through a Colin Harvey mis-kick, we ended up beating them 1-0. It was then back to Yates's Wine Lodge in Bolton for an evening of celebration. What a day!

Ray Anderson

Everton at Wembley

John lives in Ellesmere Port, and he was working in Vauxhall's with my cousin, another turner. Everton were playing at Wembley that year. Robby and John both packed their jobs up. They got a fortnight's holiday pay and a week in hand, and off they went to London. They came back with no money and no jobs, but they'd enjoyed their weekend.

Dolly Kelly

Ticket for the final of the European Cup-Winners' Cup on 15 May 1985 at Feijenoord.

Everton had a good run to the 1968 Final, but were beaten 1-0 by West Brom.

My First Trip to Old Trafford

My first ever trip to Old Trafford was with my granddad, and it was a night game, and it was the second replay of the League Cup Final when we played Villa. At the time I was at Mary Help of Christians School, and they were very strict about pupils having any time off. Quite unbeknown to my mum, my dad had written a note to the school saying that I had to attend a hospital appointment. Later in the day he picked me up outside the school in his articulated lorry. Next we went to pickup my granddad, and then we headed off down the road to Manchester. Like so many other matches that we'd been to, we could only get two seats together, and one somewhere else in the ground. So I sat through the game next to my granddad.

At the very end of the game Brian Little scored in the last minute of extra time, and that was after two replays. Granddad was absolutely devastated. We walked back across the railway lines to the car park. Everyone was dejected. What a miserable night that turned out to be. Well, that was my first experience of Old Trafford.

Karon Meehan

An Unplanned Week Away

We hired a minibus and drove down to Portsmouth to pick up some mates. We then went across to Rotterdam on the Sunday, as Everton were due to play there on the following Wednesday. Everton had a particularly gruelling week that week, as they were scheduled to come back and then face Man United on the Saturday at Wembley in the FA Cup Final. We got to Rotterdam, enjoyed the game and the trip so much that we decided to stay there for a bit longer, then head back to London and go straight to the final. That's exactly what we did. So, nine of us had left home a week earlier, stating that we'd be back straight after the game in Holland. In fact, we arrived back over a week later, having seen both the game in Holland and also the game at Wembley. Our wives weren't too pleased at the prolonged absence – especially as they knew nothing about our changed plans!

Frank Patterson

Paid for my Central Heating

A few days before we were due to meet Sheffield Wednesday at Wembley, Jimmy Gabriel rang me at home in Aintree. He told me to get down to his house as soon as possible, as he had one ticket left – and my name was on it! The ticket cost 7s 6d. I told Jimmy that I already had a ticket, but he insisted that I took this one. The only two stipulations were that I went down to Wembley, and that I didn't sell it to anybody else. He informed me that Harry Catterick was particularly keen that players shouldn't be selling their allocation of tickets. Jimmy lived at 6 Wrekin Drive in Aintree. When I got there, he insisted that I took the ticket as a present from him – not too many players would give tickets away for a

Fans on their way to Wembley.

A triumphant homecoming in 1985. Everton had won the European Cup-Winners' Cup, were the League champions and had narrowly missed winning the FA Cup.

Wembley Cup Final. I went to Wembley with Jimmy's father-in-law. Because of 1905 and 1906 when Liverpool won the League and Everton won the Cup, I was looking at 1965 and 1966 – I'm a fatalist! I looked at the 5 and the 6 again, and at the beginning of the season I put £2 on Liverpool to win the League at odds of 5-2, and £2 on Everton to win the Cup at odds of 14-1. I also had a £2 double, they were 'each-way', up and down, inside out – I covered just about every eventuality that you could think of. There I was off to Wembley to see Everton playing against Sheffield Wednesday. Liverpool

had already won the League, so the prospects were looking good. I asked my mum for a few bob so that I could 'lay off' the bets. She said, 'Change your bet, change your luck – leave it alone!'

I went down to Wembley and Dave Gaskill was sitting next to me. The chap behind us never stopped moaning. He'd given £20 for his ticket, and, at the time, Everton were losing 2-0. Wembley's the worst place in the world to get licked. Dave turned around and said, 'You've got nothing to worry about – this chap here's lost over £200!' I answered by saying that nothing was decided until the fellow in black blew the final whistle. As I said that, the ball came over and was headed down for Trebilcock to stick it into the back of the net. A few minutes later it happened again, 2-2! I was sat just opposite the Queen, and from there I could see Gerry Young, a very cultured footballer, get the ball for Sheffield. Colin Harvey had mis-cued a pass, but then Gerry Young, with all of his skill, failed to trap it. It's got to be said that the turf at Wembley that day was a disgrace. The next thing, Derek Temple seemed to come from nowhere, he got the ball and went racing away with it. He went right up the pitch like a rat up a spout, and he put the ball into the back of the net. We'd won 3-2.

A couple of weeks later I was in a bookshop in town and I saw Derek Temple but he didn't see me. I went up behind him and put my hands on his shoulders, and just said '14th May 1966, no-one can take that away from you Derek, and there are millions of Evertonians who would have loved to have scored the winning goal at Wembley.' He turned around and said, 'No, they can never take that away from me.' I asked him what was going through his head as he was racing towards the goal. He said that he was thinking about how Springett, the goalkeeper, would approach it. His answer was interesting. First he acknowledged that Springett was very cunning, and was well aware that the pitch was very heavy. That being the case, the ball mightn't have bounced over him if he lobbed it. His next thought was to take it all the way, dribble around Springett and then slot

On the way into the stadium at Rotterdam.

it home, but again, Springett would probably dive at his feet. His last thought, and the option which he went for, was to say to himself, 'It's shit or bust!' so he let fly, and it went sweetly into the back of the net. I then told Derek, that, apart from being married and having a family, that was the happiest time of my life. I'm not worried about anything else, the League, European cups – anything. Winning the FA Cup was everything to me. When I came out of Wembley at the end of the afternoon, not only was I drunk, but I was also loaded! There was enough money from the winnings to put central heating throughout the house, and it's still the same heating system today.

Frank Smith

The Priest Relented

In the 1984 Final, I took my son, who was seven at the time. I'd been taking him to the match since he was four, but he'd never been to a big game like this before. The day of the final, he was due to make his Holy Communion. Usually the service is held on a Sunday, but for some reason it was to be held on a Saturday this particular week. We went around to see the priest to try to explain that he wouldn't be there on the following Saturday, but the priest wasn't very happy about the situation. I said to the priest that we could have said that he was sick, but at least we went around and told the true story. The priest then said that he couldn't give permission, but I said that it really wasn't a question of getting anyone's permission, he was going to the game, and that was that! I

suggested to the priest that it might be the only time that he could go down and see Everton in the Cup Final – the priest immediately agreed with me, as he happened to be a Liverpudlian! In the end, the priest relented, we went to the match, Everton won, and my son took his Holy Communion at St Matthew's, Queens Drive, on the Sunday.

Dave Hughes

A Day Full of Happy Memories

This is the FA Cup Final in 1989. I was in the Liverpool half because, being on my own with some friends, we did swap some tickets. There were a few Evertonians around us, but Liverpool were winning 1-0. It got to the last ten minutes, and this Evertonian who was sat next to me suddenly shouted, 'I cannot stand to see these win again.' And with that, he went storming off. He must have got halfway down the stairs and Stuart McCall scores a goal, and then it went into extra time. Ian Rush got another goal, but then Stuart McCall scored again. Anyway, by this time, the Liverpudlians behind me we saying, 'Come on girl, cheer for them, cheer for them.' I was cheering my head off, but, no good, we still lost. But it still sticks out in my mind. It was a day full of very happy memories. It was a good score for Liverpool, as it was just after Hillsborough.

Margaret Riding

Peter Davies with Pat Nevin at Derby County.

I've Just Had My Bum Pinched

In 1986 we went to Wembley. The girls had always wanted to walk down Wembley Way, so we got the train down. So we got there, and we were at the start of Wembley Way, and I was saying to them both, 'Well here we are, we're now at the start of the famous Wembley Way.' It was two o'clock – just before the Everton coach arrived, and we intertwined all the way up, taking in the atmosphere, and when we got to the far end Jane appeared to be very upset, so I said, 'What's up?' and she said 'I've just had my bum pinched.' So I just laughed at her and said, 'Well, as long as it's not your ticket we can still go to the match.' Even to this day she still can't understand that joke.

Peter Davies

Pallets Full Of Booze

I went to the 1984 FA Cup Final against Watford. We went in one of the football specials from Lime Street. Everybody had bags stuffed full of goodies for the trip down. As the queue gradually moved forward and we were about to board the train, we noticed that there were four pallets stacked full with case upon case of beer and lager. Seemingly, some people actually thought that the police would allow them to board a 'dry' train with cases of ale tucked under their arms. They were so scrupulous that they were even unscrewing tops from flasks, and if they thought that there was whisky inside instead of coffee or tea, they were just pouring it away – what a waste! In the early Eighties, when there had been an outbreak of crowd trouble up and down

John McGovern, Chairman of Everton Supporters' Club, celebrating the FA Cup victory in the Winslow.

the country, the police adopted a policy of having 'dry' trains and coaches. It was a real anticlimax after we'd won. Instead of being able to celebrate in style, we were herded back to the train, and then it was the long journey home. By the time that we got back to Liverpool we didn't really feel like going out for a drink anyway – everyone was too shattered. It's amazing, we'd just won the FA Cup – the first time in over twenty years, and everyone was too exhausted even to have a celebration drink.

Steve Bretherton

She Didn't Find it Very Funny

In the 1983/84 season, I went to a cup game when we were playing Notts County. I got on the train with my son, David. We got to Nottingham, and were lined up on the platform and told that we had to wait for the second trainload of supporters to come in. A policewoman searched me. Then she said to me, 'And where are you going now?' I said that I was going back to the end of the queue! She didn't think that it was very funny. Unfortunately, a lot of people don't understand Scouse humour.

Stan Cain

'He'll Let you in for Nothing'

We were waiting to go up the stairs at Wembley and there was this guy hanging out of a window. He was shouting to one of his mates and I was just watching this guy for a couple of minutes whilst he was trying to attract his attention. I don't know who his friend was, but he was just shouting, 'Charlie, Charlie', and, after numerous attempts, he eventually attracted Charlie's attention. Having made contact he shouted down, 'Go to gate C, give him a fiver and he'll let you in for nothing.' It was incredible!

Peter Davies

Harry Catterick Called the Police

On one trip we arrived in Athens only to be surrounded by people who wanted to see the team. We had a

The jubilant scene after Everton's 1995 FA Cup victory over Manchester United.

coach booked to take us to the hotel, but, unfortunately, it was on the outskirts of town. We were driving along a very nice motorway when, all of a sudden, we pulled off the road and went along what was a very narrow lane. We got to a little village and then stopped. When we stopped hoards of people suddenly appeared from nowhere, and they started to rock the coach. Harry Catterick and one of the trainers got off the coach and went into the centre of the village and came back with the police. They eventually cleared the crowd, but we'd been there for over an hour, during which time we had to keep the blinds down in the coach. As soon as we started off again we were soon back on the motorway! We got to the hotel and I laid the table for the forty or so people who would be having the meal that night. I took all the linen serviettes from everyone, because I

considered that the paper ones would be much more hygienic – I wasn't going to leave anything to chance on this trip. After the meal had been served, the manager of the hotel came into the kitchen and made a very complimentary comment on the steaks – I gathered that he wanted one. So, twenty minutes later he too was enjoying a fillet steak specially flown over from Liverpool. Wanting to reciprocate, he offered our chef some stew which had been simmering on one of the stoves. I didn't have any, but the chef said that it tasted very good. We all went up to the town after everything was cleared away, and we were enjoying a quiet beer, when we could hear an almighty din coming from the vicinity of the hotel. We got back to find that there was a procession of cars going round and round the hotel – obviously trying to keep the players awake. Harry Catterick came down and called the police. They arrived half an hour later, and eventually shifted the cars, but not with any enthusiasm. The next thing, another half-hour later and there was a circle of motorbikes going round and round the hotel. Once again the police were called, and once again they eventually moved the motorbikes away. The last act came at one o'clock in the morning when about one hundred people had gathered, and were singing at the tops of their voices – what can you do about that? There was more to come however. The next morning, the chef couldn't 'turn to'. He'd been bad in the night as a direct result of eating the stew – I had to cook breakfast for forty people on my own!

Ken Davies

Villa Park in a Clapped-out Mini

I used to play football when I was at university, and there were a couple of guys that I was quite friendly with – they also played football and were keen Everton supporters. One day, quite on the spur of the moment, one of these guys suggested driving down to Villa Park to watch Everton play in a cup game. So, at five o'clock in the evening, four of us set out for Birmingham in a clapped-out Mini. It really was clapped-out, having only one seat, and that was the driver's. The three of us in the back just sat on the floor, trying to steady ourselves as we were hurled around corners and roundabouts. We got there and managed to get some ground tickets. The night was wet and

Enjoying the atmosphere at Rotterdam in 1985.

Another special occasion in 1995 – this time celebrating Dave Watson being voted Player of the Year and Everton winning the FA Cup.

miserable. I can't even remember whether or not we won, the memory that is uppermost in my mind is being wet, miserable and having to endure a very uncomfortable drive back to Manchester.

Karon Meehan

The Captain Sang over the Tannoy

When we went to Holland in 1985 for the European Cup-Winners' Cup, we took a couple of coaches from the supporters' club. The match was on a Wednesday. Some coaches set off on Tuesday morning, but the coach that I caught didn't leave until Tuesday evening. We travelled overnight to Holland. We then had a smashing day

there, just looking around and absorbing what was an absolutely electric atmosphere. The Dutch seemed to welcome us far more than our opponents' supporters – Rapid Vienna. We had a great day and an even better result – we won 3-1. Coming back, everyone commented on what a good, well-behaved crowd of supporters we were. When we got on the boat shortly after one o'clock in the afternoon on what was a glorious day, everyone was milling around, but then all of a sudden there was an urgent announcement asking for our attention. Everyone stopped what they were doing and began to listen. It was the captain himself on the Tannoy. My first thought was that somebody had blotted their copybook, but it was nothing of the sort. The captain said that the announcement was for everyone and in particular all of the Everton fans. He went on to congratulate the supporters for their exemplary behaviour, even saying that they'd been ambassadors for both their club and their country – but most of all for their country. He finished off by singing the current Everton song over the Tannoy – 'Here we go....'

Jim King

The Green Man

I remember The Green Man in 1977 when we played Aston Villa in the League Cup. It was the first time that we'd had anything to celebrate for years. At the time Liverpool were winning just about everything that there was to win, and this was our first real break. We'd already beaten Bolton in the semi-final over two legs. Peter Reid had his leg broken by George Wood, the Everton goalkeeper. We travelled down to Wembley en masse and there were Everton supporters all over the place. They must have come out of the woodwork from just about everywhere. When we got to London we went into a pub called The Green Man, it's not too far from the ground. We started to play five-a-side football outside the pub against Villa fans – it was all very good-natured. There wasn't that much to commend the actual game itself, as it was a 0-0 draw. The replay was at Hillsborough, and on that occasion the result was 1-1. Our next replay was across at Old Trafford, but this time we lost 2-3. Still, we'd had a good try.

Tony Riley

I Took my Cousin from Barbados

I went along to the FA Cup Final against Liverpool, and I took along my cousin from Barbados. I also took one of my sons. In 1984 I'd been over to Barbados on holiday and met one of my cousins for the first time. The following year he came over here with his wife. I went down to Wembley with my son, and we met my cousin at the stadium. Unfortunately, we didn't have a ticket for him, and we weren't able to buy one. The three of us joined the queue, and when we got to the turnstile we just pushed, and we all got through on two tickets instead of three! As we were going up the steps there was all this pee on the floor. You may remember, it was a fine sunny day. My cousin asked where all the water was coming from, and I had to tell him that it wasn't water but pee! He didn't believe me. He then went on to tell me what happened when he went to a cricket match at the main stadium in Barbados. I said, 'When the cricket ground's full and you want to go to the toilet what do you do?' He said, as though it was really quite a stupid question to ask, 'Well, you just make your way out to the toilet.' He didn't really seem to understand my question. It seemed so obvious to him that when you wanted to go to the toilet you just went along! I suggested that if he could find his way to the toilet and then get back to the same place at Wembley then he wouldn't be doing that bad. He just couldn't understand this aspect of English life. I went over to Barbados again the next year, and my cousin was still telling all of his friends how he had been 'stowed away' at Wembley.

Leo Skeete

It Was Ruled 'Off'

I went to a game in 1977 when Everton were playing against Liverpool. I think it was the semi-final of the cup which was being played at Maine Road. I think that it was the game when there was a controversial goal disallowed. Hamilton scored for Everton, but it was ruled 'off'. The atmosphere was great – I even went across to the game with some Liverpudlians. What did frighten me, however, was the police horses outside. We were just walking along into the game, and these horses were coming along at a bit of a canter, and that was a bit scary. The police seemed to over-react a little bit.

Peter Spear

A 'blue' and a 'red' – brothers Iain and Andrew Hadwin, leaving home for the 1986 Cup Final.

Merseyside At Wembley

I went to the Milk Cup, the first all-Merseyside final at Wembley. We went from the Eagle and Child in Halewood – I used to play for their Sunday League football team. We arranged to meet there at six o'clock in the morning. Everybody was well prepared, having at least twenty-four cans each for the day. Next, the manager came out of the pub carrying a big hold-all jam-packed full of bottles and cans. Also, some of the lads had bottles of spirits – one guy was even having a swig of gin straight from the bottle, and then having a swig of tonic from another bottle – and remember, this was still six o'clock in the morning! When we got to Wembley itself, little dividing walls separated us. I was in one section, and most of my mates were some distance from me in one of the other sections – there were police all over the place. I was drinking a can of lager at the time, and I started to climb over the wall in order to be nearer to my mates. All of a sudden a policewoman came along and asked me what I was doing. Having explained, she then actually held the can for me as I climbed over the wall. She happened to

71

comment that, in all her time at Wembley, this was by far the best match that she'd ever been to – the atmosphere was electric.

The game ended 0-0, and was not the most exciting of finals, but I didn't get home until three o'clock in the morning! The whole day was a good experience. The coach was a fifty-odd seater – half of the fans on board were supporting Everton, and the other half were supporting Liverpool, but everything was in good spirit – everyone enjoyed themselves that day.

Steve Bretherton

It Spelt Out E V E R T O N

When we were playing against Rapid Vienna, we arrived at the ground well before the match was due to start. The first thing that we saw was seven guys lined up in white boiler suits, and each of the suits had a big blue letter on the front. As they stood in line, it spelt out E V E R T O N. We waited outside for a little while, and then decided that it was time to make our way into the ground. Unfortunately the police were funnelling us through one gate, which meant that there was quite a crush to get in. Just then, one of the gates fell down and there was a surge forward. The guy in front of me who had his young daughter with him fell to the ground. We managed to pull them along with us until they were out

EVERTON F.C.
Europacup II 3e ronde 1985

VAK
H

Onoverdekte staantribune f 10.—

Verkoop en/of afgifte van dit toegangsbewijs geschiedt onder de door de KNVB op 15 augustus 1984 bij de Arrondissementsrechtbank te Utrecht gedeponeerde algemene voorwaarden, welke verbindend zijn voor koper en/of ontvanger en mogelijke opvolgende houder(s) dezes.
Op aanvraag te tonen.   Z.O.Z.

Ticket for the Third Round of the European Cup-Winners' Cup against Fortuna Sittard. Everton won 5-0 on aggregate.

The 1976/77 FA Cup semi-final against Liverpool.

F.A. Challenge Cup 1976-77
Semi-Final
EVERTON v LIVERPOOL
Saturday, 23rd April 1977
Kick-off 3.00 p.m.

You are advised to take up your position
half an hour before the kick-off

BLOCK **1**   ROW **39** SEAT   80

BLUE - REAR
Platt Lane £3.50

Secretary

TO BE RETAINED (SEE PLAN AND CONDITIONS ON BACK)

of danger, and could stand on their feet again. They would have been trampled on otherwise.

John Kelly

Where Did You Get that Hat?

I'd never been to Wembley before, so there was no way that I was going to miss that game [in 1966], especially after what I'd been through to watch the semi-final. But, the lads that I went to the match with, local lads gradually dropped out one by one. But I still wanted to go. Anyway, through the tannery where I worked, I met another guy who wanted to go to the Final. There was a pub in Bootle, the Coronation, and they had a coach going on the Friday night. We were booked on the coach, even though we didn't have any tickets. I was twenty-one at the time. When we got on the coach everyone was drunk and they were all fighting. It was the longest journey of my life. It took over eight hours, because we kept having to stop at just about every single services. People were falling asleep in toilets and we'd have to go looking for them – it was a rough journey to say the least. We eventually got to London shortly after seven in the morning and found somewhere to eat. We then had a wash and brush-up before starting our search for tickets. We couldn't find tickets anywhere. We eventually went to a pub and started to ask in there for tickets – nothing! Even the Sheffield Wednesday supporters were very friendly in the pub, but we still couldn't secure any tickets. We went down to Wembley and tried to give some money at the gate, but we were 'back-heeled'. And there I was in my special top hat that the girls in the tannery had made especially so that they could see me on the telly. All I could hear was the crowd inside cheering and then starting to sing *Abide with Me*, as they always do – but I wasn't part of it. I'd come all this way, and there I was stood on the steps outside. I decided, in desperation, to have one last try. I went up to a turnstile and gave the guy a pound note. Immediately the turnstile opened and I was in! I couldn't believe it. The steps were right ahead of me, so I climbed up and saw the players shaking hands with Princess Margaret. I raised my hands in the air and gave a shout of triumph. It was short-lived. Just then I felt a hand on my shoulder. On turning round, I found that it was a copper. He asked for my ticket, but I said that I'd just been to the toilet. He retorted by saying that I hadn't been past him. How could he forget the hat? It was then that he agreed with me, and said that as he couldn't forget it, he knew that he'd never seen it before. I was frog-marched to a group of Wembley officials. I told them my story, but they were having none of it – even though I gave what I considered to be a bravura performance. A policeman escorted me out of the ground. As we were walking out, and with a few drinks inside me, I decided that it was now or never. I made a run for it! I took off with my hat in my hand, running as fast as I could. I ended up in the Sheffield Wednesday area, but I didn't mind. A guy who'd seen me running had a spare seat next to him – he signalled to me

and I sat next to him for the remainder of the game. From that day to this, I'm convinced that the copper didn't chase me, but I didn't stop to look back! When I eventually plucked up courage to look at the game itself, the first thing that I saw was Jim McCalliog putting the ball in the back of the net for Wednesday. But, after going 2-0 down, we came back to win 3-2, as everybody knows.

Ray Anderson

The Best Five Pounds I've Spent

The 1966 Cup Final, I went down but I didn't have a ticket. I went down on the 7.30 train. All my friends had tickets, so they were happy – I was the only one in our group not to have a ticket. But, from what my Kopite friends had told me, all I had to do was to put a pound on the turnstile and I'd be through. I got there well before the turnstiles opened, and waited for the first one to open. I was the first customer. I calmly placed a one pound note on the counter and the turnstile operator looked at me and indicated that there was nothing doing. I went along to the next turnstile, and there was a policeman standing outside. I put my pound on the turnstile. The man behind asked me to move away before he called the police. The same thing happened a few times – so I decided that I needed to up the stakes. I dug deep and fished out a fiver. Going back to the turnstile with my bluey, I was told to clear off in no uncertain terms. I couldn't sort anything out. Nobody had any spares for sale. But then, at twenty to three, this old chap came wandering over. He gathered a small group around him, so I tagged along to see what was happening. He gave them one ticket for the game – the only one that he had. The five Everton lads didn't know quite what to do, so, without too much hesitation, I swapped my five-pound note for the ticket. I suggested to the lads that they should go along to the pub down the road where the match was being shown on a big screen – at only one pound each. I said that they would all be able to see the match by taking that solution. I was away before they could change their minds. As I walked in, the band was just beginning to play *Abide with Me*. It was standing room only. My parting memory of Wembley that day, when we won, was being arm in arm with a gang of Liverpool dockers and doing the hokey-cokey. That five pounds was the best money that I've ever spent in my life.

Jim King

Towed Home after the Match

In the early Seventies Everton were playing West Ham in a semi-final match. The game was at the neutral ground of Villa Park on the Saturday afternoon, and my dad was lucky enough to get some tickets for us. The only problem was, there were very few coaches going down to the match, and all the ones that were going were booked up anyway. So, not having a car at the time, my dad asked around all his mates to see if he could borrow a car for the day. One of his best friends said that he could borrow his car. The great day

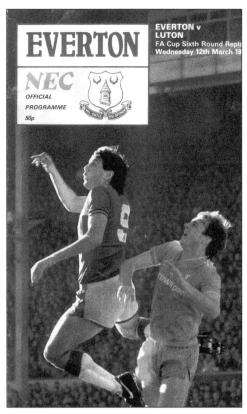

Programme for the Cup replay against Luton in March 1986.

came, the car was delivered in the morning, and we set off in style for Birmingham. Unfortunately we lost the game, so I didn't get to the Cup Final that year.

On the way back, feeling fairly dispirited, as we were odds-on favourites to win this game, the car broke down. It was unbelievable. There was steam coming out of every conceivable orifice, there were also some very nasty noises coming from the engine compartment. Dad looked under the bonnet, but there was very little that he could do at the time. Dumping the car on the side of the motorway, we hitch-hiked as far as the next services, and then started to phone around all of our friends to see if anyone could come out to tow us home. This was a tall order for a Saturday night, but one of my dad's friends drove down in a pick-up truck and towed us all the way back to Liverpool. We then had to face the owner. He promptly informed us that the car had broken down the week previously. It was a complete write-off. It was an awful end to an awful day.

Karon Meehan

My Leg Feels Wet

In 1986 I went down to the FA Cup Final. It was summertime, and a particularly warm day. Four of us went down by car – our Paul, Julie, our Raymond and me. Because it was so hot, I was just dressed in shorts and a T-shirt. We got down there in good time, parked the car, and got the Tube a few stations out to this working men's club that we'd been told about. We went in and it was amazing. There must have been upwards of 200 people from Halewood in this particular club. As soon as we walked in, it was just like walking into the Leather Bottle – we knew everyone. Unfortunately, somebody pinched a jar full of money. We had a whip around and raised over £200 – more than double what was in the bottle anyway. People were laughing and joking. It was a great atmosphere. Some people even had blue shirts and red scarves on, or vice versa.

When we got to the ground, with me stood there in my shorts and shirt, I could feel my leg getting warmer and warmer. Unfortunately, it was also getting wetter. The fan next to me was

peeing down my leg! He couldn't get to a loo and just had to go! There was nothing that either he or I could do.

Steve Bretherton

The Bolton Wanderers Semi-final

Dave Hickson was a great favourite at Goodison. He was a fearless centre forward. There wasn't a lot of him, but what there was, was absolutely superb. I've got some tremendous memories of him. Do you remember Matthew's year in the Cup Final, '53? Well, that year Everton got to the semi-final, and we were playing Bolton Wanderers at Maine Road. Even then, Hickson was a legend at Goodison. We'd beaten Man United in one of the earlier rounds that season, and when we were playing Bolton, Hickson practically won the game on his own. He was swathed in bandages, as he'd had a few knocks during the game. At one point he was taken off, but he came back, and fought his way through the defence to put the ball in the net. It's games like that one that stick in your memory. In that particular year in the semi-final, when the great Nat Lofthouse was playing for Bolton, there was a chap called Malcolm Barras, a big centre half, a big yard-dog as we called him, and the first time that Hickson went for the ball, Barras charged into him. Hickson recounted later that he couldn't remember too much about the first half of the game – he was absolutely finished. Anyway, Everton came back from 4-0 down at half time, to be 4-3 at full-time. They even missed a penalty in the second half! And that's how we

Another trip to Wembley, this time to see the 1984 Charity Shield game against Liverpool.

went out of the Cup on that particular occasion.

Larry Lynch

The 1966 Cup Final

My elder brother asked me if I wanted to go to the 1966 Final but, for various reasons, I couldn't go. Watching the game on television was an absolute nightmare. Very quickly Sheffield Wednesday scored a goal. Everton had lots and lots of chances and the unfortunate Jimmy Husband just seemed to keep missing every opportunity. Everybody was having a bad game and then disaster: 2-0 for Sheffield Wednesday. I remember going out of the front door into the street, tears in my eyes, and a few of the other local lads, we were all Evertonians, were the same. We tried to console ourselves by buying lolly ices for each other. We came back, and Everton staged a most fantastic comeback in the second half. Mike Trebilcock scored, at which stage we all ran out, arms in the air, acknowledging the achievement. Then Trebilcock equalized – unbridled joy in the street. And, when Derek Temple flashed in with a fantastic run and shot to make it 3-2, our joy was beyond measure. For the rest of the game we sat outside with our hands over our ears because we couldn't bear the thought of Sheffield Wednesday getting a late equalizer or winner, and when the final whistle went, there were more jubilations.

Nick Hawkins

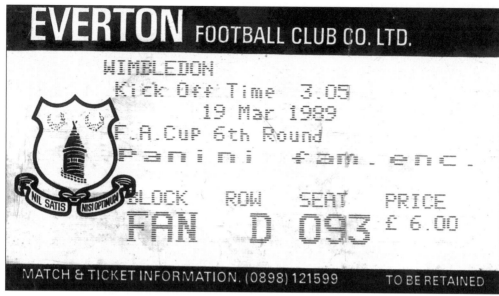

EVERTON FOOTBALL CLUB CO. LTD.

```
WIMBLEDON
Kick Off Time  3.05
        19 Mar 1989
F.A.Cup 6th Round
Panini  fam. enc.

BLOCK    ROW    SEAT    PRICE
FAN       D     093    £ 6.00
```

MATCH & TICKET INFORMATION. (0898) 121599   TO BE RETAINED

Ticket for the Sixth Round of the FA Cup against Wimbledon.

Lukewarm Orange Juice

When we played Panathinaikos at Goodison we put on a big buffet and there was as much drink as anybody wanted. The buffet included everything that you could think of with Scotch salmon, lobsters, turkey, beef, salads etc. There was no expense spared – they were treated like royalty, because John Moores had told us to look after them, and we did. When we got over there it was a different story. I shared a taxi to the game with John Moores. When we got to the stadium, there was no one there to greet him, and the seats that we had been allocated left a lot to be desired. It was a sports stadium where the team was playing, and there was a running track all around the perimeter, so we were a long way from the action on the field. There were rows of loose chairs where we were sat. During the course of the game, the chairs were moved all over the place. To make

matters worse, it hadn't rained out there for months and months, so the pitch was bald and hard as a rock, nothing like the superb playing surface that the Everton players were used to in England. Something else which wasn't like being at home was the cordon of soldiers around the perimeter of the field who were all carrying sub-machine guns. We didn't see much of the match. When the match was over, we made our way over to the main stand area. All the players were in the showers, and we were just waiting for them so that we could catch our flight back. During the whole of the time that we were waiting for the players, nobody approached John Moores to offer him a drink or any other form of hospitality. The only thing which we were given was a glass of lukewarm orange juice at half time.

Ken Davies

Ticket for the 1989 FA Cup Final against Liverpool.

'Women Shouldn't be at Matches'

This was an Arsenal-Everton semi-final in the Littlewoods Cup, first leg, and I took my cousin who was only nine at the time, as he just wanted to go to a football match. We were walking across to the ground, and I happened to be just in front of an Arsenal supporter, just in his way, and he started – 'Women shouldn't be at football matches, you know nothing about football.' Well, that was it, I let him have it, I really did. I said to him, 'What do you mean? I probably know more about football than you.' In the end a policeman came over and suggested that I should just ignore him and walk away – so I did.

Margaret Riding

Straw Hats on the Pitch

My early recollections of matches is somewhat jumbled going back all that time, but there's one that I do remember, and it's the 1933 Cup round against Luton. It was the sixth round, and all of these Luton fans, the 'Hatters', came along with their boaters on – we called them straw gutties in Liverpool, because all of the business people used to wear then in the city. They came up in tram-loads and it was the first time that we'd realized that there were so many people going to away matches, because they could be identified by the straw gutties. We won 6-0, and when the match ended, they all took off their straw hats and threw them onto the pitch. There was then a

Everton supporters on Wembley Way before the 1995 FA Cup Final.

mass invasion, whilst we scrambled to retrieve them. They were of very good quality, with soft kid leather inside, and a leather strap that could be clipped into your buttonhole so that the hat didn't bow away in a high wind. Funnily enough, years later I happened to be in New York, and I got chatting to this guy – another Evertonian. He said that he remembered the match, not for the scoreline, but for the hundreds of hats which were strewn over the pitch at the end of the game.

John McGovern

Tears of Joy and Tears of Relief

I first started going to the match in 1971, the year after we won the League – my dad took me, as I was only nine at the time. He went with me until about 1975 when I decided to go on my own. The Seventies were a pretty barren time for Everton, and I'd never seen them win a trophy, so when they got to the League Cup final in 1977 against Aston Villa, that was it for me. There were three games, but, as everyone knows, we were beaten in the third one. It was the first time that I'd ever cried watching Everton. Unfortunately, it was the same year that Liverpool won the European Cup. It was a great disappointment for me. After that there was another quiet time until 1984 when we got to the FA Cup Final against Watford. Most of the people that I was with all the same age as me, and like me, they'd never seen Everton lift a trophy. But, when Ratcliffe picked up that trophy there were floods of tears coming down my face. I looked over to where I could see Howard Kendall, and there were tears coming down his face also. I felt quite embarrassed, but when I turned around, there were blokes all around me and everyone of them had tears in their eyes – tears of joy, tears of relief to actually be winning a trophy after so long.

Bob Maylor

This chap dropped his crutches, retrieved the ball and kicked it back with his broken leg. Unfortunately, because of this, and the fact that he wasn't on his crutches any more, he went flying to the ground. The crowd thought that this was hilarious. We were in bulk!

John Kelly

We Were in Bulk

When we played against Rapid Vienna in Holland, the area behind the goals was empty – this was to help with crowd control. Anyway, they let one guy stand behind the goal, as his leg was in plaster. All of a sudden, the ball came over the back of the goal.

Officials of the Everton Supporters' Club at the 1995 Player of the Year Evening.

CHAPTER 4
Our Players

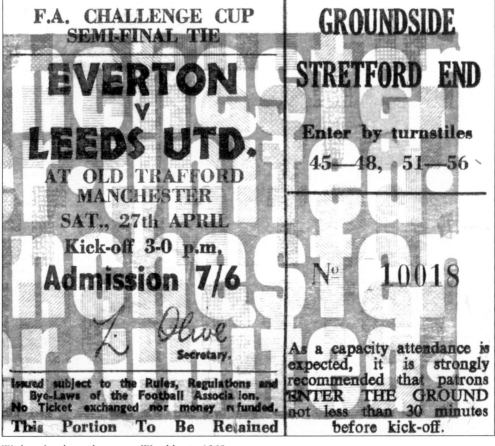

F.A. CHALLENGE CUP
SEMI-FINAL TIE

EVERTON
v
LEEDS UTD.
AT OLD TRAFFORD
MANCHESTER
SAT., 27th APRIL
Kick-off 3-0 p.m.
Admission 7/6

Olive
Secretary.

Issued subject to the Rules, Regulations and
Bye-Laws of the Football Association.
No Ticket exchanged nor money refunded.

This Portion To Be Retained

GROUNDSIDE

STRETFORD END

Enter by turnstiles
45—48, 51—56

Nº 10018

As a capacity attendance is
expected, it is strongly
recommended that patrons
ENTER THE GROUND
not less than 30 minutes
before kick-off.

We beat Leeds on the way to Wembley in 1968.

Thirty Goals in a Season

Do you remember when Bob Latchford scored thirty goals in the League – the first player to do so? Well, I was at that game in the Gwladys Street end. It was a penalty, and Latchford had to score either a hat trick or two goals in that game to reach the record and it was the last game of the season as well, so there were all kinds of bets riding on it. You could see guys all around sweating on this, and when the penalty came, and he was taking this kick, they opened up all the back gates in Gwladys Street, so all the kids who normally just listen to the game outside were actually allowed in to watch this little bit of Everton history. Anyway, he got his thirty goals, and it was absolutely superb. I don't think that Everton actually won anything that particular season, but no doubt achieved, yet again, mid-table respectability. At least we could boast the leading goal-scorer in the League, and that was pretty impressive.

Karon Meehan

George Burnett in the Park

When we went to play football in Litherland Park, George Burnett often used to walk by our pitch. He lived in that part of Litherland. Even though he was always dressed immaculately, he'd sometimes go in goal for us. This was in the days of the great Eglington and Stevenson – two of the giants of the game.

Harold S. Scott

No Fags!

Even our own players took some barracking; in this case it was Johnny Morrisey, the Everton winger, who was well-built, like a tank. The rumour was that he and an ex-Everton goalkeeper had been involved in getting hold of some cigarettes, how shall we say, not quite legitimately. So not only did Johnny Morrisey have to cope with running down the wing and getting tackled by centre-halves and murderous-looking full backs, but he also had to endure the chants of 'Have you got any fags, Johnny?' This was every five yards or so. And finally, when he got fed up of this, he'd turn to the crowd and say in a loud voice, 'No, I haven't got any ******* fags.'

Nick Hawkins

He Scored in the 91st Minute

On Grand National day in 1995 when Kanchelskis was playing for Everton, we were playing away to Blackburn. It was at the end of April. I didn't go to that particular game, but I placed my bet as usual. I always do a bet for Everton to win 2-0 at away games – it's just one of those traditions, or maybe superstitions. I've lost so much money it's unbelievable! We were in the pub just watching the National, and I had this betting slip in my hand. I'd put five pounds on Everton to win by 2-0, and the odds I was given were 25-1. We were in the Black Horse, and it came up on the television screen, with just five minutes to go, that Everton were winning 1-0. I screwed up the betting

EVERTON
FOOTBALL CLUB
CO. LTD.

OFFICIAL TEAM SHEET

Football Association Challenge Cup
FOURTH ROUND

SUNDAY, 27th JANUARY, 1974 at 2-15 p.m.

EVERTON		WEST BROM.
Blue Shirts		Yellow Shirts
White Shorts		Blue Shorts
David Lawson	1	Peter Latchford
Terry Darracott	2	Gordon Nisbet
John McLaughlan	3	Ray Wilson
David Clements	4	Len Cantello
Mick Lyons	5	John Wile
John Hurst	6	Alistair Robertson
Mike Bernard	7	Willie Johnston
Mick Buckley	8	Tony Brown
Joe Royle	9	David Shaw
Gary Jones	10	Asa Hartford
Joe Harper	11	Allan Glover
	12	

Referee : **Mr. J. D. WILLIAMS** (Wrexham)
Linesmen : **Mr. G. W. A. HESPE** (Sheffield) Orange
Mr. A. BRADLEY (Accrington) Cerise

40p.

Retain this Team Sheet—it may help you to
obtain tickets for future Cup Ties.

The team sheet for the first ever Sunday game at Goodison.

slip and threw it into the bin. The next thing that we heard was that Kanchelskis had scored to make it 2-0. I dived into the rubbish bin to rescue the betting slip – people had been throwing cigarette ends, chewing gum, empty crisp packets, and all sorts of other things into this bin, but I did manage to find the ticket. I phoned my cousin Laurence and told him to get ready for a night in town as I'd won over a hundred quid. I went down to the betting office, just by the Glebe, and put the slip in. The girl behind the counter was pleased for me, as she too was an Everton supporter. She was just about to cash the slip when the manager's hand came over and stopped her from taking the money from out of the till. He informed us that the game had kicked-off ten minutes late, and he couldn't pay out the money until the final whistle was blown. Disaster struck – Kanchelskis scored in the ninety-first minute to make the final score 3-0!

James Harrison

That Goal Put us Through

The most memorable season that I can remember at Everton Football Club was in 1984 when they won the FA Cup. It was a season when we were coming out of the bad old days, but the skies were still grey. One of the most memorable games that I can remember that season, and there were lots of them, was the day that Andy Gray scored the diving header at Notts County. I was standing under a stand that was leaking. I was soaked through, it rained from the minute that we kicked off, right through to the end of the game. There was just a complete torrent and downpour, but the way Andy Gray applied himself on that day was great – it's certainly a day that I'll never forget. He was only about six inches off the floor when he headed in – it was one of the best goals, if not the best goal that I've ever seen. That goal put us through into the next round of the cup.

Lawrence Santangeli

Brian Harris Walked in

When Everton played Swindon Town in the cup in the Seventies we went into a pub after the game, and guess who walked in – Brian Harris. He got the biggest cheer of the day, and everyone went over to him and asked him if he wanted a drink. I seem to think that he was living down that way at the time. The Everton players have always been very close to the fans.

Joe Harrison

A Great Day

It was a great day when we signed Kanchelskis. He was one of my favourite players, and I always enjoyed watching him. But he left Everton before too long. I think that it must have been about money, but I'm not too sure. He played an important part in what is still my favourite game. We actually won 7-1 and he scored either two or three of them. Gary Speed also got two that afternoon.

Anthony Skeete (aged 13)

'Your Tiny Hand is Frozen'

There'd been some discussion in one of the papers about who had the largest hands – was it Sagar in our goal, or Swift for Manchester City? Anyway, we were playing this game on a very cold afternoon. For some reason I recall that it was a two o'clock kick off. Somehow, Sagar fumbled the ball and let it go into the net. Immediately, our resident trumpeter who used to stand in Gwladys Street kicked off with *Your Tiny Hand is Frozen*. The following evening he was

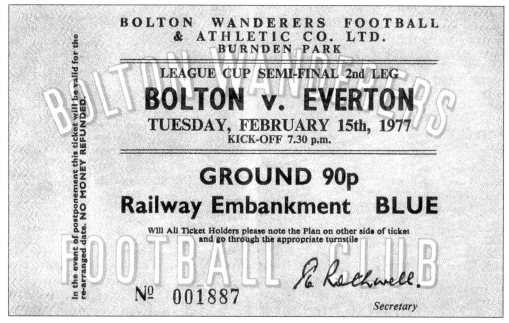

The 1977 League Cup semi-final against Bolton. We won 2-1 on aggregate.

featured in Derek Green's cartoon in the *Echo*.

John McGovern

A Great Gary Stevens Fan

Jane was a great Gary Stevens fan and one night after the game she said, 'Can we stay behind and get Gary Stevens' autograph? I know him very well, and he knows me.' So we waited and it was freezing – it must have been three below. After we'd been waiting for ages I got fed up and said that I was going. Anyway, we walked up City Road, and Peter Reid came out. Anyway, behind him there was Gary Stevens and, remarkably, Gary looked

Mike Milligan at Bellefield.

up and said 'Hello Jane, how are you?' And he walked straight across to her – they were on first name terms. I just couldn't believe it, I nearly fell over. I said, 'Jane, I thought that you were only kidding me.' It's often the way that players let on to people, but they really were on first name terms.

Peter Davies

My Favourite Player

I first started to go to the matches when I was about fourteen. My favourite player was Graeme Sharp. He was gorgeous, and very much my hero. He always seemed to have the ball, and he was always there when you needed him. Later on, I enjoyed watching Gary Lineker – I still love to see him now when he's talking about football. When I first got a season ticket I used to sit in Gwladys Street, but now I'm in the stands. I enjoyed Gwladys Street better because there seemed to be more atmosphere.

Joanne Harrison

How's My Niece?

A girl I used to be friends with was as mad about Liverpool as I was about Everton. Sometimes she'd come to Goodison with me, so I used to go to Anfield with her. She was mad on Kenny Dalglish and his attitude. So I used to tell her that Colin Harvey had the same sort of approach. In fact, I always thought of him as a sort of uncle of mine. He just seemed to have that

Winners of Duncan McKenzie's shirt – another charity 'do'.

sort of character – I was only seventeen at the time. Everything we spoke about was football, and I'd often say to her, 'I saw Uncle Colin the other day,' and comments such as that. One night we waited behind after the match to get some autographs and it was freezing – we'd waited for hours. Then Colin Harvey came out and started to walk across the car park. We ran across shouting, but he didn't hear me at first, so I shouted even louder, 'Uncle Colin, Uncle Colin.' but then I realized what I'd been shouting when he turned around. I apologized, but he just laughed when I explained the story. After that time when he came out he always used to say, 'How's my niece, is she doing alright?'

Faye Davies

I Fumbled to Put it Back

One day after a match, I'd been invited into the players' lounge to have a drink with Paul Rideout – I have to admit that he was very much my number one hero at the time, and I was a little nervous about meeting him. When I got there he hadn't arrived, so I decided to have a cigarette to calm my nerves before he came from the changing room. Just as I was about to light up, his young son informed me that his dad hated smoke and smokers. I immediately fumbled to put the cigarette back in its packet! I met Paul on several more occasions, and he was a very charming man.

Anita Gallagher

Ian Snowdin with his daughter Zoë.

The All-round Centre Forward

Tommy Lawton came in the thirties
and, in my opinion, Dean was past
his best by then. He played with Lawton
in the late thirties in the same forward
line, but I always believed that Tommy
Lawton was the all-round centre
forward, he was the better of the two.

Larry Lynch

Is It Really Mrs James?

I remember Jimmy Gabriel when he
first came to Everton. He'd married a
girl called Pat Gaskill, and her father
was a good friend of mine, and Jimmy
was playing for Everton when we won
the League. It was the first time that
we'd won the League since I'd been

supporting them – and that had been for
quite a few years. I wasn't an Evertonian
because they were winning, I was born
an Evertonian, and I watched them
from 1947 right up to 1963. I was made
up when we won the League.

In the 1965/66 campaign Jimmy was
still playing for Everton, and wherever
they were playing I sent him a telegram
in every round of the Cup. One week he
was injured and he couldn't play.
Believe it or not, he was checked into a
women's ward in the name of Mrs James
– this was so that his hospitalization
wouldn't become public knowledge. The
telegram was sent to Sandy Brown. We
were playing Manchester City on that
day, and we haven't got a particularly
good record against them. Well, we won
2-0, and I remember saying that if we
can win there, then we can win
anywhere. We then got to the semi-final

and we were due to play Manchester United. The match was played at Bolton. I'd never seen Everton win the FA Cup, and I desperately wanted them to win that year – it was like a mania with me. We were beating Man U. 1-0, and all of a sudden I got a terrible pain in my gut, and I couldn't stand up to watch the game. Sid Hughes, who was the secretary of the police club in Fairfield, was looking at me sitting on the floor. He wondered just what was wrong with me. I told him not to worry about me, but to tell me when the ball was in their net! By this time most of the United fans had gone home because Everton were winning. Things didn't improve when Sandy Brown wellied it into the stands, but it didn't matter that much. The result was 1-0 for us, and we were on our way to Wembley.

Frank Smith

Are You Playing Today?

I was in the Blue Bell the other week, me and my missus together with another couple, and Eddie was at the bar. Just as we were making our way to the bar, someone shouted over to him, 'All right Ed, did you go to the game today?' The answer, which came in a flash, 'They won't bloody kick off unless I'm there!'

Tony Riley

Everton's Greatest Ever Captain

One recollection is about Everton's greatest ever captain, Kevin Ratcliffe – and I say that with every respect to Dave Watson. At the time Kevin was the manager of Chester City. I happened to be in Chester doing a bit of Christmas shopping with an ex-girlfriend of mine. The place was packed out, and I just saw him there in the middle of the shop with his wife. Nobody seemed to know who he was, but I did. I walked straight over and asked for his autograph. He seemed a bit embarrassed, but asked me what I thought of the game over the weekend. I told him that Everton had played well, but he was talking about how Chester had played!

James Harrison

Mike Newall at Manchester City.

John Bailey with adoring fans at the Player of the Year ceremony.

Dean's Comeback in the Reserves

I can remember going with the old man to Goodison. Dean had broken his leg and he was making a comeback in the reserves. I think it was before 1933 when we won the Cup, but I can't be sure. But at Goodison Park on that day, you'd have thought that there was a First Division match going on, because of the crowd that turned up to see Dean make his comeback after breaking his right leg. When they were kicking in before the game started, he hit a shot with his right foot, and he hit a cracker right into the net. Well, the ground just erupted – you'd have thought that he'd scored the winning goal at Wembley.

Larry Lynch

Well-established Internationals

During the war, my formative years, both Everton and Liverpool were playing in the Northern Premier League. We used to play teams such as Notts County and Stockport, and a lot of the players were in the Army and stationed in this part of the world. There were always lots of players 'guesting'. It wasn't unusual to see some really well-established internationals playing for Everton.

Harold S Scott

Dave Hickson was a Great Idol

Dave Hickson was a great idol of mine, an icon – he's still working at Goodison now. When he got transferred to Liverpool it broke my heart, and my dad said, 'Don't go to watch Everton any more.' I remember his debut when he scored two goals against Aston Villa. During the Easter holiday period, I went up to the training ground with a friend of mine, and we were collecting autographs. Not being familiar with the training methods, we were trying to look for players and ask for their autographs. I always remember Dave, because he was training on his own. He'd gone into the pavilion and changed his footwear – I didn't know this at the time. He was doing some sprinting. When I asked him for his autograph he was very offhand with me and just said, 'I'll sign whilst I'm sprinting shall I?' That upset me, but I suppose that the guy was only doing his work, he was just coming back from injury as it happens. There was my idol shouting at me. Anyway, I carried on collecting autographs but I was a little downhearted. After the training session had ended, I was still collecting autographs from some of the other players. Then Dave Hickson came out and a crowd swarmed around him to get his autograph, but I didn't go. I stood to one side, and, when he'd finished signing for everyone he came over to me. He apologised for shouting at me, but explained that he had to complete his schedule. I felt ten feet tall, there was my idol apologizing to me! I've never forgotten that day, and I've never lost that enthusiasm.

Peter Davies

He Always Missed Everton

Faye was on speaking terms with Gary Stevens through knowing him from getting his autograph, and when he moved from Everton up to Scotland, he would sometimes send tickets down to her, or leave them somewhere for her, and she would travel up there to see him play. He always missed being at Everton.

Mary Davies

Farrell Played his Heart Out

I can remember the days when Everton always used to hover close to the Second Division. I remember one particular season when Peter Farrell was playing for Everton, and he always gave 100 per cent in any game – he just didn't know how to play half a game of football. He was quite a marvellous person from that point of view. Later, when Everton actually went into the Second Division, I was there on the Saturday afternoon for the final game of the season when they had to beat Blackpool to stay up. Unfortunately, and I really can't remember whether it was Stoke or Blackpool – poor old Everton didn't pick up the points and went into the Second Division. Matthews was playing, and it was the one time that I'd seen him playing on Merseyside. Other than that you never saw Matthews, but on this particular Saturday, I remember being in Goodison Park and Matthews played. On that day Farrell played his heart out trying to stem the tide, but all to

Ian Snowdin with young Rachel, aged four.

no avail – the damage had been well done by then.

Harold S. Scott

He Didn't Figure in the Plans

Stuart McCall is one of my favourite players, so when we signed him I was delighted. My big disappointment is when he scored two goals against Liverpool, but he still came out on the losing side. We'd also signed Peter Beardsley, and I know that he was looking forward to playing alongside him, but Kendall had other ideas. He virtually told him [McCall] that there was no place for him in his new team. He suggested that he spoke to Rangers, as he didn't figure in the new plans for Everton. I was away on holiday at the time, but when I got back and heard the news, I rang my dad. I was in tears at the time, I just couldn't believe that he'd gone. He was supposed to be coming to my eighteenth birthday party, but he rang me and said that he couldn't come. He wrote me a letter saying how sorry he was because he couldn't make the party. After he'd left my mum went off right Kendall, as he'd upset me so much because he'd got rid of McCall.

Faye Davies

A Teddy Bear for Mr Jackson

During my first lecturing position at a university college, I undertook some additional teaching. It was for the Chartered Institute of Marketing, which, being a marketer, presented no major worries. However, little did I

EVERTON FOOTBALL CLUB CO. LTD

GENERAL MANAGER C.S. BRITTON ════════ SECRETARY W. DICKINSON

Telephone
AINTREE 2263

Telegrams
FOOTBALL LIVERPOOL

NIL SATIS NISI OPTIMUM

GROUND & REGISTERED OFFICE:
GOODISON PARK
LIVERPOOL · 4

OUR REF   YOUR REF   DATE

6th July 1953

Mr. P. M. Chamberlain,
778, Longmoor Lane,
Liverpool. 10.

Dear Peter,

       Training recommences on Tuesday,
21st July 1953 at Bellefield, West Derby, from
6 p.m. onwards and will continue on each subsequent
Tuesday and Thursday evening throughout the
season. As in previous seasons we will hold the
training sessions at Bellefield while the light
nights prevail, transferring to Goodison Park
later on.

       There is still a shortage of training
gear and if you could possibly bring your own it
would be appreciated. However, if you are short
of any item of kit we will endeavour to fix you up.

       Looking forward to seeing you on
July 21st and I trust that the coming season will
be a happy and successful one for you.

              Kind regards,

              Yours sincerely,

C. Britton

A letter to Peter Chamberlain inviting him to attend a training session at Bellefield.

know that after accepting to teach on this programme, I would be teaching a group of professional footballers – nine in total. I had sportsmen from the lower divisions such as Crewe and Preston, but also Mr Watson and Mr Jackson from Everton. Mr Jackson's wife was expecting their first baby at the end of the first term, so during the whole of November he used to bring in his 'bleeper' into class. Anyway the baby finally arrived without disrupting the sessions. I asked Matthew if he could get me some tickets to watch Everton in December for my dad's birthday. Of course we went but suffered a 2-0 defeat against Newcastle. To show my gratitude I posted Matthew a lovely

teddy bear with a red scarf on for his new son. Little did I know that they were Liverpool colours on the bear. Oh dear – I might be able to teach, but I obviously knew nothing about colours!

Yvonne Moogan

'Stalking' Graeme Sharp

I remember going to 'stalk' Graeme Sharp. He lived over towards Ainsdale/Freshfield way. Me and my friend were waiting for him to come out of his house so that we could get his autograph. We waited for ages behind the bushes, but he didn't come out. We were both totally infatuated with him. We loved him and the way he played.

Joanne Harrison

Graeme Sharp was on the Train

We went down to Arsenal recently. They beat us 1-0, and Graeme Sharp was on the train – he goes down to do match reviews. He was sat there with his wife and kids, and all the fans started to sing 'There's only one Graeme Sharp.' He was nearly in tears when he realized that the fans still thought so much of him all those years later. He stood up and thanked everyone. His wife and children were obviously feeling very proud of him.

James Harrison

A benefit night for Mark Higgins in 1984. Higgins' injury robbed him of winning honours with Everton.

Peter Beardsley enjoying
Linda's company.

Cliff Britton was Outstanding

My father often used to talk about
Cliff Britton – he was a real
gentleman, as well as being an
England international. My father
insisted that he could dribble a ball
right along the by-line, and I always
tried to do this, even though the ball
was too big for little feet. Many years
later I heard Cliff Britton speak at
Liverpool Methodist church. He was
an outstanding man who lived a very
circumspect life. He was an absolute
credit to Everton Football Club. He
was universally appreciated
throughout Merseyside.

Harold S. Scott

Eddie Wainwright

But then of course Lawton came on
the scene – he was the greatest all-
rounder that I've ever seen as a centre
forward. It was in late '45 or early '46,
one or the other, the war had just
finished, and I was still in the Navy –
I hadn't been demobbed at that time –
I wasn't demobbed until '46. I was on
leave, so I took my young brother to
Goodison, we were playing Fulham,
and a lad named Eddie Wainwright
had made his debut not long
beforehand. He was a tremendous
prospect. Joe Mercer was playing right
half – we played with positions in
those days – and Alex Stevenson who
was a great inside left, but happened
to be playing on the right wing for
Everton, linked up with Eddie
Wainwright, and Mercer was the

A happy Neville Southall after a successful training session.

prompter behind them. Wainwright scored five goals that day, and Everton won 10-1. The significant thing is that Fulham had fielded three full internationals that day. I thought to myself, 'Everton have got something on their plate today.' Wally Boyes was playing left wing – he was a player who'd come from West Brom and he turned Fulham's internationals inside out on that particular day. As I say, Mercer was prompting and Eddie Wainwright scored five.
Unfortunately, I think that it was the following year that he broke his leg and that more or less finished his career. He was a tremendous prospect.

Larry Lynch

Neville Got Things for People

Neville Southall came out to the school where I work. Neville always got things for people – shin guards for kids and the like. I went to him and asked him if there was any chance of a pair of boots – I was just being cheeky. He said that he'd get me a pair, but I thought that I'd be waiting at least six months. At the very next game I saw him coming in, and he said that I should go over to the main reception. I went around to reception after the game and was presented with the best pair of boots that I've ever worn in my life, there wasn't a break in them – really good boots. I got a couple of seasons out of them. A few years later I was playing in a game at Bellefield and I happened to leave the boots in the dressing room. I was told that the boots had been returned, and that I could pick them up from reception. Needless to say they weren't there. I saw Neville and told him the story about the boots which still had his initials on them. He looked around in his pigeonhole but couldn't find them. Realizing my predicament, he said that he'd send someone down to the training ground to have another look. They couldn't be found, so, directly after the game he went straight back to the dressing room and produced another pair of boots which he then presented to me. I've still got those boots.

Peter Davies

Dave Hickson's Head

All I can remember about the first game that I went to at Goodison was the sight of Dave Hickson's head. I was about five at the time and my mum was a Liverpool supporter, but there wasn't that much talk about football in our house in those days. Anyway, a chap from across the road – Lenny Cruikshank, who's now an OBE, took me along to the Boys' Pen. There were plastic season tickets then, and some people put them in their mouths and flicked spit all over the place – a disgusting habit. But my main recollection is watching Dave Hickson. I don't know who we were playing, I can't remember the score, but I can remember the head of Dave Hickson. From that day I became an Everton supporter – just because it was the first game that I ever went to. At

that time Everton were in the ascendancy. We often used to go to Everton one week and then we'd go to Liverpool the next week.

Leo Skeete

CHAPTER 5

League Games

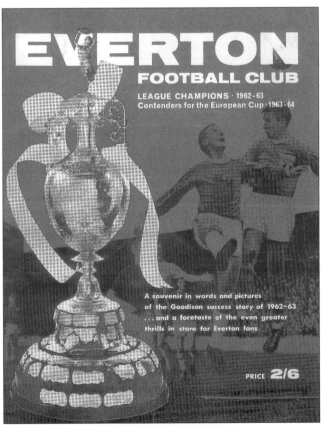

Everton Football Club – League Champions, 1962/63.

Turning The Tables on Liverpool

And then there was our first derby win after seven years, and that was one of the occasions when I had to go to the game on my own, because at derbies you just got tickets for anywhere in the ground. Unfortunately, I couldn't sit anywhere near either my dad or my granddad who were both ardent Everton supporters. Anyway, I got this ticket, and mine was in the Gwladys Street stand; my dad had a ticket in the main stand. It was the time when you wore the shirt, I was really obsessed. So I walked to the match, and, as most of my friends were Liverpool supporters, I walked along with them. All the way to the game they were taunting me, suggesting that this would be the eighth season when Everton were not able to overcome Liverpool. So I became resigned to the fact that we were unlikely to do anything, but if we could get a draw it would be some sort of bonus.

When we got into the ground it was absolute chaos, because people had been bribing the men on the turnstiles, so there were thousands more in the ground than there really should have been. I managed to get my seat, but there were bodies all over the place. Well, Andy King scored this absolutely fantastic goal. I couldn't believe it. I didn't even bother getting the bus home that night, I walked all the way home, and the smile on my face stretched from ear to ear. A truly great night for Everton, and one which I'll never ever forget.

Karon Meehan

Beaky'll Make It Better

One of the legendary incidents that I can remember from the 1970s was the sort of banter that used to go on between the crowd and certain players from other teams. Generally speaking, the more of a nuisance or good the player from the other team was, the more they got mercilessly barracked by the crowd. I remember one incident in particular. There was this enormous docker in the Gwladys Street end who kept barracking Mike Summerbee from Manchester City, using such expletives as 'Here comes Beaky', 'Go and smell your way home', 'He'll pass it with his nose' – you get the general picture, and Summerbee was having a particularly poor game anyway. Just after half time, Summerbee raced for the ball near to the corner flag, beat about two men, and then just fell over as he was about to pass to Colin Bell. Well, of course, the large docker, string vest and all, couldn't resist saying, 'There you go Beaky, you can't even pass the ball five ******* yards.' Next thing, showing the tremendous athleticism that only comes to somebody who is particularly cheesed off, Summerbee vaulted over the wall, ran up to our docker friend, hugged him, kissed him and uttered the unforgettable line, 'There, there, Beaky'll make it better.' This caused great merriment in the crowd. He then jumped back over the wall and went on playing. He wasn't barracked for the remainder of the game.

Nick Hawkins

Moving towards the League title.

Beaten 10-4 by Tottenham

My earliest memories of Everton go back to that time when we were beaten 10-4 by Tottenham. I was still at school and my sympathies had always been with Liverpool because my dad was a Liverpudlian, but after that match I switched allegiance to Everton. I don't know whether you remember, but there was a programme on television called Highway Patrol, and their call sign was '10-4'. Everton and Everton supporters took a lot of stick over that score! I used to go along with some lads from school. Fortunately, our results became a bit better after that drubbing. In fact, we went on to win the League in 1963. I remember going to the final match of that season – I think we either beat Fulham or Cardiff 4-1 when Roy Vernon scored a hat trick. I remember the atmosphere, it was just fantastic to be there when they won that championship. It was nothing like it is today, it seemed to be in a lower key. The players didn't make as much fuss as perhaps they would today. Everything seems to be a business now. I've met Brian Labone a couple of times, and he would have pulled on an Everton shirt for nothing, he was so pleased to be turning out for the team – but that sentiment doesn't seem to apply any more.

Peter Spear

Our First Match

Our first match was against Sheffield Wednesday, and it was about eight matches into Joe Royle's reign, and we hadn't conceded a goal under him until then. The date was 26 December 1994. We scored first, early on in the game, but we ended up getting beat 4-1. It was a real shock, Guy Whittingham scored two that day I think. The next match was against Ipswich, and we won that one 4-1, so it was an indifferent start to our watching Everton.

Andrew & Anthony Skeete (aged 15 and 13)

We Beat Plymouth 8-4

I remember a couple of games in particular, but I'm talking about over forty years ago, so my recollection mightn't be exactly as the games were at the time. I seem to remember that at one of the very first games that I went to we beat Plymouth 8-4. I remember that Plymouth played in green shirts with white sleeves. That was very unusual, even in those days – teams never played in green, for fairly obvious reasons. The other thing that sticks out in my memory about that game in particular was the fact that one of their players had a beard, and in those days football players just didn't have beards! Another game that I remember, also one of my first games, was the game against Rotherham when we drew 4-4. When I went along to those first few games, I got the impression that every game had about ten or twelve goals, but that isn't the way of football! I'm not sure about those scores, but that's the way I remember them.

Malcolm Hadwin

A Goal-Line Scramble

We had Alex Young, and he was a magic player. I can remember being at one of the derby games at Goodison Park when Liverpool had Yeats and St John – it was that era. I was sat by a family of brothers, and all the brothers had daughters, and their one sister had a son. So on this day the brothers had brought along their one nephew to watch the game. They'd taken him to the match in the hope that he would become an Evertonian. There was a goal-line scramble, and somehow Yeats managed to let the ball go over the line, but the ref didn't award the goal. I was dead in line with the goal line, and it certainly appeared to be a goal as far as I was concerned. The ball was in the back of the net, but the referee blew up for a free kick to Liverpool, right on their goal line. Back to the brothers who were sat next to me – every time the ball got anywhere near the Liverpool goalmouth, the little boy wanted to go to the toilet. Manfully, the brothers took it in turn to escort him to the loo. I suppose that they must have only seen about 70 per cent of the game. The game as I remember wasn't that exciting – in fact, it was more entertaining listening to the family next to me!

Harold S. Scott

They had Met the Night Before

I remember about twenty-six years ago, before I was married, when my future wife and I went down to visit friends in South Wales. I had known Len for many years and whilst Chris (my future wife) had met him, she had never met his wife Irene. We travelled down to Wales on the Friday night after work and, early the next day, Len and I travelled back up to St Andrews, Birmingham, where Everton played Birmingham City in a League game. We left the girls, who had only met for the first time the night before, on their own for virtually all the Saturday. It's a good job that they liked each other and the weekend was a success. There was, however, one snag – Everton lost 1-0 with a young Trevor Francis scoring the only goal. Notwithstanding that weekend, or maybe because of it, Chris and I got married and after the wedding went away for a week. Everton were playing at home on the Saturday so I had to make sure that we got up early that day to travel back home in time for me to get to the match. I don't know whether Chris would stand for that now!

Peter Spear

I Can't Listen to Crucial Games

I still get so 'worked up' about football – I can't listen to some of the crucial games. Last year when they stayed up, they had to win, but they still didn't know whether they'd stay up or not. We were playing Coventry and Bolton were playing Chelsea. I didn't listen to the first half. My daughter was listening, and she told me that Everton were winning 1-0 and that Bolton were losing 1-0. If both games ended like that, then we'd be OK. I started listening to the second half, and we were still winning. It was getting on for the end of the game when my next door neighbour knocked on the door. He'd brought me a bottle of wine to congratulate the fact that we'd stayed

up. He thought that the game had finished, but the match was still going on. As I took the wine Coventry equalised! I couldn't believe it. If Bolton equalized in their game, then we'd be on our way down. Fortunately, they didn't.

Peter Spear

It Was Worth Every Penny!

This happened the season before last when we very nearly got relegated. My nephew, who lives in Sydney, Australia, had been making regular phone calls to see how our team were doing. We arranged for him to give me a phone after the final whistle of the last game. Sure enough, just as the whistle was being blown, my mobile phone started to ring. I was able to tell him that we were still in the Premier League, and then left the phone on while he listened top the roar of the crowds. In fact, I left the phone on all the time while I went over to the Winslow for the celebration champagne which we drank after the game. All this time, Paul was still on the line. I was crying, he was crying in Australia, and just about all of the fans around me were crying by this time. In all, he must have been on that phone for over half an hour – but it was worth every penny!

Brenda Clintworth

Dicks Out

Julian Dicks was playing for West Ham, and we were just sitting there watching the match. He came over by

Trevor Steven converting one of his two penalties of the afternoon. Everton went on to win the League Championship that year.

us to take a throw in, and all of a sudden, this chap next to me started to chant with much fervour, 'Dicks out, Dicks out, Dicks out.' The chant was soon taken up by the crowd. Eventually, around the ground, everybody was chanting, 'Dicks out, Dicks out, Dicks out'. It sounded very funny that night on telly.

Tony Riley

The Old Man Was Demented

I remember, because I was at the game, when Liverpool beat us 7-4 at Anfield. That was the game in 1933, the year that Everton won the Cup. The team that Everton won the Cup with was the team that they put out against Liverpool that day, with the exception of one, Albert Geldard wasn't playing – Ted Critchley played on the right wing. Dean scored a couple I think that day, but a fellow named Tommy Barton scored four for Liverpool, and Liverpool only had a gang of youngsters out that day. The old man was demented, I was only about seven or eight years of age at the time.

Larry Lynch

What a Relief!

The last game was against Coventry, so my brother who lives in London came up for the day. He brought a mate over from Belgium, and also two of his other mates that I'd met before. My other brother, who still lives in Liverpool, also came along to the game. We were absolutely convinced, like most other people on Merseyside, that this was Everton's last season in the Premier Division. Bolton were playing Chelsea, and we were playing Coventry – Chelsea didn't care, and we were resigned to a tormenting time. We went along, and it was like a wake. We went out first thing in the morning, and we were drinking all day, but the stupid thing was, nobody was drunk. We were all too sombre to be anything other than sober. Before the game we met in the St Hilda's. Before that however, I'd been physically ill in the morning, I just couldn't deal with the situation. I always take my eldest lad along to the game with me, and he just couldn't understand what was going on. I kept apologizing to him for being in such a sorry state. Eventually there were about ten of us in the pub, all feeling miserable and dejected. I just wouldn't wish that feeling on anybody, even my worst enemy. All the Liverpudlians were celebrating our demise, but I was just too overcome with grief. Even my mate, who's over six foot tall, was feeling very

sorry for himself. Just before we went into the ground he broke down in tears, and started to apologize to all of us. One of the policemen who was at the ground tried to console him, but he was in rather a sorry state, and somehow beyond gentle words of consolation. The atmosphere when we went into the ground itself was incredible. It was like being at the funeral of a close member of the family. The fans around us were all feeling the same as we were. But, as everyone now knows, we didn't go out of the Premier League that day. What a relief!

Tony Riley

We Jumped over the Turnstile

I remember one League game at Maine Road, about twenty-odd years ago, when Rodney Marsh was playing. I went with Malcolm an old friend of mine. We were delayed, there was a big crowd, and the match had already started by the time we got to the turnstile. We were told that the ground was full, but a £5 note to the man on the gate allowed us to jump over the turnstile and get into, I think, the Kippax Stand. Malcolm and I made our way with great difficulty, squeezing past everyone else to two seats right behind the goal and in the middle of the stand and, just as we sat down, very relieved to be in, everyone else in the stand stood up. City had scored. What a start to the afternoon.

Peter Spear

Programme for the Everton *v*. Chelsea game, November 1986.

Banned For Twelve Months

My daughter was banned for twelve months after the Arsenal game at Highbury, and that's going back about five or six years now, and all for the simple reason that she turned around to have a go at them because they were throwing cigarette ends at her. She was arrested by a policewoman and charged with being drunk and disorderly, and was fined £80 by a woman magistrate and was banned from attending games for twelve months – she hasn't been to a match since. She's a really fanatical Blue, both home and away. Away supporters seem to be treated like cattle these days.

Stan Cain

The 1970 League Title

When we won the League in 1970 against West Brom I went to that game with my brother Vinny. At the time I was thirteen and he was only ten. When we won, and the score was 2-0 just for the record, the official attendance at the ground was just over 68,000, but I reckon that it was nearer to 80,000. Harvey and Whittle scored, and it was great to see the ball going into the back of the net. As we were only small, we were lifted over everyone's heads and carried down to the front. It was a good game, and we had a good vantage point – one of the best under the circumstances.

Tony Riley

We've had our Ups and Downs

Of course, we've had our ups and downs like any other football team. The biggest one that I remember was in the late Fifties, or maybe the early Sixties, and that was the Purple Hearts fiasco. We had an away game at Anfield, and this chap ran onto the pitch, and stuck a huge Purple Heart on a stake into the centre spot. We went on to beat them 4-0. I don't know whether that was the spur or not, but it certainly worked for us on that occasion.

John McGovern

The Sound of Silence

Before progressing to the Gwladys Street end, via the Boys' Pen, my first visits to Goodison Park were with my father. We would go with my 'uncle' George and his son who lived near to the ground in Pinehurst Avenue. The time I'm talking about is when boys still carried boxes (usually beer crates) to stand on, in one hand, and wooden rattles in the other.

Whether it was by design or coincidence, I'm not sure, but we always seemed to go on the Saturday when Everton were playing Tottenham Hotspur. It seemed a noisier game in those days less sophisticated, less analytical, more an opportunity to stand in a cold amphitheatre and shout at the top of your voice. My mum always knew when I'd been to a game as I usually came back with a sore throat and only a whisper for a voice.

During these early games with Tottenham

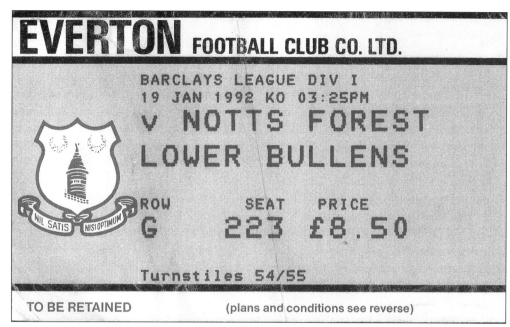

Ticket for a League game against Nottingham Forest in the 1991/92 campaign.

there occurred the strangest phenomenon, which at my tender years I could not fathom. I just knew something was different. During certain periods in the game, amidst all the chanting and mayhem the crowd would suddenly fall silent. It was as if a conductor had raised his baton, or that we were observing the armistice silence after a Boys' Brigade church parade. Looking down onto the pitch to see what was happening and if there was any reason for this curious crowd behaviour, there would be a little Spurs inside forward on the ball, jinking past my beloved boys in blue as if they were toy soldiers.

In all my time of watching football matches I've never experienced the chilling silence one player could have on a game or stadium, but then there will always only be one Jimmy Greaves.

Colin Paul

We Fought Back to Force a Draw

One of the things that I think that my dad would agree with is that Everton like to keep you hanging on – both result-wise and performance-wise. For instance, we were going to West Ham, it was the 1996/97 season. We'd been travelling since early that morning and we'd had a few cans on the way down – there were one or two other Blues with us on the trip. Anyway, we got to Euston. I've been to London quite a few times, but I always seem to get mixed up in the Tube. We generally leave all those sort of arrangements to one of our mates, Michael Keene. We just follow him, especially when we've had a few pints down us. We were meeting a few other mates in a pub just by Victoria station. We got to the Nelson, as agreed, only to find out that Liverpool who'd been playing United that day had just been beaten in their twelve o'clock kick-off, so

Selhurst Park Stadium

FA CARLING PREMIERSHIP
WIMBLEDON V EVERTON
SAT 03 OCT 1998   KICK OFF 15:00
ARTHUR WAIT STAND
BLOCK U   ROW 29 SEAT 79
PRICE £20.00   VISITING SUPPORTER
ENTER VIA ENTRANCE 5

O.A.P.

Ticket for the Arthur Wait Stand, October 1998.

we had something to celebrate right from the start! We made our way to West Ham, having a few more drinks before we went into the game. Just before half time we were 2-0 down – Everton were playing awful. Paul Kitson, who'd already scored two goals, stepped up to take a penalty. Everyone agreed that, if they scored a third, then they would leave the match and go out for a night on the tiles in Soho. Neville Southall, who was having a great game, actually saved the penalty. We were relieved, and thought that our fortunes may now change. There was forty minutes left in the game, so we decided to stay on in the hope that we might be able to turn the game. We made a substitution, and scored shortly after. Everyone was hoping that we could somehow manage to score another before full time. Ferguson, from a cross from Barmby, took a superb diving header to equalize. There were celebrations all around the ground. And to think, forty minutes before I'd been ready to leave the game in disgust. There

was Laurence, Michael Keene, David Doran and his brother Tommy, and me, and we decided that it was celebration time. From being 2-0 down, we'd fought back to force a draw. We walked back to the station ready to catch our train home at about half six, but we ended up missing the train. By this time I only had ten pounds left. We borrowed some money from one of the lads and then made our way to Soho. We ended up kipping down on a hotel room floor. The room was cramped, but at least we had somewhere to sleep for the night. It ended up being a great night. But that's Everton – they always keep you hanging on right until the last minute!

James Harrison

CHAPTER 6

Other Times

Brenda Clintworth with two of her grandchildren.

Everton v. Crystal Palace – Wembley, 1991.

The Afternoon Party

In 1979 a rather attractive woman invited me to a party. I thought, strange, as the party was only due to last during the afternoon. Anyway, I went along, and went into this room which was absolutely filled with beer, sandwiches and other tempting morsels. I just couldn't believe it. Also, lined up along the opposite wall were most of the Everton first team players. They seemed to be having a complete ball, getting completely and absolutely smashed out of their brains. It was hilarious. There was dancing, singing and lots of other unbridled exuberance. The players were great. They were chatting with everybody at the party and giving autographs. Everyone, including me was well away that day. Unfortunately, I had to leave to stagger back and do some

work. Suddenly, a stunning thought hit me – a few days later, Everton were due to play in the quarter-finals of the FA Cup. I'm glad to say that we won.

Nick Hawkins

He Really Knew Nowt About Football!

I took a mate to his first match about three seasons ago. He really knew nothing about football but he was coming down from Leeds especially to see the game. I paid for his ticket in the stand, picked him up at Lime Street, took him for a pint and then took him to the game. He loved every minute of it. At half time I nipped out to get some tea. When I got back there was no sign of him – I couldn't see him anywhere. I spent the rest of the game looking for him, just in case he was lost in the crowd. After the game I spent another hour looking around all of the pubs by the ground, just to see if I could see him there. In the end I thought I'll go home, phone the police and also inform his family. I got home and found him sitting on the doorstep. When I asked him what the hell was going on, he told me that, at what he now realized was half time, he'd seen the crowds leaving, and thought that the match was over. When everything had been resolved, he then had the cheek to complain about the lack of commentary during the game!

Paul Lucas

His Father Played for Everton

As a young boy I'd made friends with all the boys that I went to school with, and I remember one particular lad in our school whose father actually played for Everton. It was good to think that you had a friend whose father played professional football for Everton. We were only nine or ten at the time, and it didn't really have that much impact on us – not in the same way as it no doubt would for youngsters today. He was just another dad with another job. There wasn't the celebrity that now accompanies all Premier League football players. I first started going to football with my father, but later on, when I was a little older, I was allowed to go on my own. I can remember that we used to go straight up the road to Stanley Hospital

Vincenzo relaxing in a Greek temple – a new fan of Everton from Palermo.

Zak – a Blue since the day he was born!

and then up Carisbrooke Road and then right into Goodison Park. The thing that sticks out in my mind was that all of the players always appeared to be much older – but now, fifty years later, they don't look that old at all!

Harold S. Scott

I was More Interested in Football

In 1970, Everton were playing Chelsea in the Charity Shield – the 'opener' to the season. It wasn't played at Wembley in those days. In fact, that year it was being played down at Chelsea. At the time Kay, my wife, was expecting one of our children. I was chivalrous, first taking her to the hospital, and then heading on down to go to the game –

that was it! I was accused of being more interested in football than my own family. I wonder just how many men have had that accusation thrown at them?

Joe Harrison

I Was Mortified

Many years ago now, I was driving through Formby – it's an area that I don't know very well, as I don't often get there. I was looking for some familiar landmarks, when I had to negotiate a bend in the road. As I came around the bend, I realised that there was a pedestrian crossing in front of me, and of even greater significance, somebody had just set off across it. I jammed on the brakes and came sliding to a halt almost on the crossing itself. The man on the crossing turned around and gave me such a meaningful look. When I realized that it was Bob Latchford I was mortified. I don't know whether he lived in Formby, but he was certainly there that day.

Heather Jarvis

We Let them Buy the Full Bottles

When we staged the matches for the World Cup, I had the massive car park at Goodison covered with canvas, and there was a huge marquee there. We put a big counter there, and all of the foreign visitors came through by the park and into this area. We built a big outside staircase which went up to the Gwladys Street stand. We were still selling spirits at that time, but it was mainly whisky that we sold. Everything was sold from the optics. At one game there happened to be quite a few supporters from Norway, but they didn't want to buy measures of whisky, they wanted to buy the full bottles! In the Bullens Road stand there were three canteens, which is where these Norwegian people were. They just wouldn't settle for the measures that we were serving, so we let them buy the full bottles. There were thirty measures in a bottle, and they bought the whole lot – there certainly was a good profit made that day! There was no trouble. Because there were going to be a lot of foreigners at the games, I decided that we'd better offer coffee as well as the usual assortment of drinks – we'd never sold coffee at Goodison before then. The volume of sugar that we got through was unbelievable, some people were putting four or five spoonfuls into their drinks. I've never known any group of people with such a sweet tooth. We also did lots and lots of different types of sandwiches. The whole venture was very successful.

Ken Davies

It was Heart-breaking Leaving

We were sailing out of Liverpool one Christmas morning. Christmas Day happened to fall on a Thursday that year, and Elder Dempster Line always sailed out on a Thursday, and returned to the port on a Saturday. We used to get shore leave from the Saturday to the Thursday. In those halcyon days, teams would play on Christmas Day and then again on Boxing Day, providing that it didn't fall on a Sunday. We were just leaving our berth, when we saw this crowd of people queuing up to get the tram to Goodison to watch the game. It was heart-breaking leaving the city that day.

John McGovern

He'd Seen Them Win the FA Cup

We got to the Cup Final a few years later, but my dad didn't want to go back – he'd been there once, and that was all that he wanted to do. He'd seen them win it once – he died in 1981. He was quite happy to be able to say that he'd seen Everton win the FA Cup.

Malcolm Hadwin

They Might Fit Me!

I went to the games regularly throughout Everton's bad period. Liverpudlians would say that this lasted for ever, but Evertonians would say that it lasted between about 1971/72 and the mid 80s. During that time we tended to have a very direct style of play with Mike Lyons typically up front, all hustle and bustle. I suppose that the entertainment value of some of the games wasn't particularly high, which put you more in mind to enjoy a few drinks at half time. One day, having had a couple of cups of beer, because they served beer in cups in those days, I went back into the crowd and started to attempt to eat this pie. As I bit into it, I felt that it was quite hard, and I wondered what it might be. So, peeling

Everton Football Club Co., Ltd.

Registered Number 36624 England

Manager:
G. F. LEE

Secretary :
J. GREENWOOD

Telephone
051-521 2020

Ground and Registered Office :
GOODISON PARK
LIVERPOOL
L4 4EL.

Telegraphic Address :
"FOOTBALL" LIVERPOOL

Dear Season Ticket Holder,

As you will be well aware Mr. Lee in winning the Manager of the Month title for November has been awarded a gallon of Bell's Scotch Whisky and he expressed the wish that this should be supplied in miniatures and distributed to some of the many loyal Evertonians who have also contributed to the Club's success.

I am happy to advise you that as a result of the ballot amongst our Season Ticket Holders you are invited to come along to Goodison Park on Tuesday next, December 13th, between 6.30 p.m. and 7 p.m. when Mr. Lee will be pleased to present you with a miniature bottle of Scotch as a gesture of thanks for your support.

Please present this letter to the Commissionaire on the Directors' Entrance. If you wish to watch the Everton v. England (Youth) fixture afterwards a ticket will be provided.

Yours sincerely,

J. GREENWOOD

Secretary.

To Dave
Best Wishes
Gordon Lee

Gordon Lee didn't drink – so, when he won the Manager of the Month title, and the scotch that went with it, there was a ballot in order to share the proceeds.

back the pastry, I found to my horror both palettes of a set of dentures stuck into the pie. A man in his late forties who was stood next to me noticed my look of amazement, and, without pause for breath said, 'Give us them lad, they might fit me!' This was typical of the sort of humour that you got on the terraces at that time.

Nick Hawkins

He Got Some Biscuits out for Us

One night, a Wednesday night, there'd been a game and afterwards we went off to the Paradox night club – it's disco night on a Wednesday. David Unsworth was in there with a friend of his and we were chatting to him, because we knew him from being at the matches. I went to the bar to get some drinks and I'd been waiting for some time. One particular barmaid wouldn't serve me – she was going to all of the men first. So I stood there trying to get some attention when she went and served somebody else. I called her over and said that it just wasn't on. This guy looked over at me and it was Graeme Stuart – I felt so embarrassed. Anyway, I went over and explained that I wasn't being funny with him, but that it was just the attitude of the barmaid. Some time later he came over and joined us when he was being hassled by some young girls. We had a really good night. When we left they asked where they could get a taxi. We gave them a lift home instead, and they invited us in for coffee. He even got some biscuits out for us – he really was very pleasant. People often think that players take advantage of young girls, but he was really very pleasant to us. We often saw him after that. He

was such a nice person.

Faye Davies

We'd have Done the Treble

I firmly believe that if we'd have played the FA Cup Final before the European Cup-Winners' Cup Final, then we'd have done the treble that year. The other thing that really annoyed me that year was that we won the League and we won the European Cup-Winners' Cup. We then got to Wembley and got beat 1-0 against Manchester United, and Norman Whiteside scored the goal. We then bought him and he only played for us for a few minutes, or it seemed like, and then he never played again. But what really annoyed me that year was that Granada put on a two-hour programme showing United

Middlesbrough *v.* Everton, September 1998.

coming home. The Cup's great, United are a great team I have to admit, but we'd been in the Final, we'd also got lots of other silverware that season, but we didn't get a mention on that programme.

Bob Williams

An Evertonian Ever Since

I went to a school in Scotland Road, and we got bombed out during the war, so we moved up here to Walton. I used to travel by tramcar down to school every day, and in those days there was a School Board – in effect, the truant officer, and they used to come round quite often. Anyway, the one that was appointed to our school was a Liverpool player, a chap called Cyril Done. He was a centre forward. We were in the habit of going to see Liverpool one week, and then the next week we'd go along and watch Everton. We had no particular preference at that age – we were only eleven or twelve at the time. One day Cyril came to the school and he was chatting with the headmaster. I mentioned to some of my mates that he was in the school and that we should get his autograph. Within a few minutes four of us went trooping off to the toilets. On the way back we waited at the bottom of the stairs, knowing that the great man would be passing by at any minute. Sure enough, a few minutes later he came down the stairs. We stopped him and asked for the four autographs. Straight away, without apparently giving it a second thought, he marched us straight back up the stairs and into the

headmaster's room. He then suggested that we were four malingerers, and proceeded to bawl us out in front of our classmates. We were all given the stick, and resumed our seats feeling somewhat aggrieved, and not a little sore. We all resolved, there and then, that if that's what Liverpool players were like, then we would be Evertonians – and I've been an Evertonian ever since!

Jim King

Her Legs Were Red Raw

When Jane was a teenager she used to go to every game that she could. Because it was the teenage fashion at the time, she never ever wore tights or socks in those days, and she'd come home on a Saturday with her legs red raw. Hail, rain or snow – they'd be standing there for hours on end, her and her mates, waiting to get autographs. Even her brown leather bomber jacket, which she got when she was about thirteen, has just about every autograph on it. She won't part with it, it's still here now and she's twenty-seven!

Mary Davies

Fourpence to Get In

The first games that I went to see were the wartime matches. There were no stands open because of the war. I used to go in the Boys' Pen in the Bullens Road end where it was then. It was 4d to get in, and I used to go with one of my brothers who's eighteen months older than me. We went to see

Peter Reid giving the benefit of his advice to young fans.

a match one night, which was a combined team of Everton and Liverpool – they were known as Liverton, and were playing against North Western Command. The game was in aid of the Lord Mayor's Fund. We were debating what the team colours would be, because of the fact that it was a combined team. In the event they were in blue because it was being played at Everton. Our home side won 4-1, and the goal scorers were all from Everton. There was a centre forward, Cecil Wyles who scored three and Wally Boyes scored the other one. He was a left winger who used to play alongside Alex Stevenson. They were great days for football. You saw players who were applauded onto the field as well as off. During the war we watched either Everton or Liverpool about once every month. We weren't able to see any of

the sides from down south, as there were travel restrictions. All the leagues were altered. There was the northern section and the southern section and whatever. But times have changed that much now, it's just unbelievable. If my dad was alive today he'd never recognize either of the grounds.

Stan Cain

An Hour and a Half Before

I started watching Everton when they were in what was then the Second Division. I can't remember much about individual games, but what I do remember is the fact that I used to go along with my dad. The Boys' Pen used to be in the corner of Goodison Park, Gwladys Street. Obviously it was

Father and son anticipating a good game at the 1984 FA Cup Final.

the other side of the park. We always had our tea there, and my dad used to tell her all about the game that we'd just seen. That was one of my most vivid memories of my early days of supporting Everton.

Malcolm Hadwin

Not Interested in the Wedding

All I can tell you about myself is that my husband is a red hot Liverpudlian, and with my family it's a religion – you had to be Evertonian. I had two brothers, and when I started courting Harry, they said, 'You're not serious with that bloody fellow, are you Dolly?' So I said 'Why?' and they suggested that I should change my religion – and they meant it! People were like that in Liverpool in those days. What made matters worse, was the fact that he was a season ticket holder at Anfield. They couldn't get season tickets for Everton. Anyway, the day that we got married Everton were playing Liverpool in a cup-tie. Of course, you can imagine, we didn't have a television, and there was a bridal car and two other cars – we lived in Belmont Road then, we were only going around the corner to the church, St Margaret's. We lived in Whitefield Road, and there's not very far to go to the ground. So they were asking the driver to take them along to the match. We eventually ended up in our house where we were holding the wedding reception, as was the way in those days. We didn't have a television, but there was a wireless. Everyone just gathered

cheaper to go into the Boys' Pen. In those days it was open behind, but later on they fenced it off. Dad pushed me into the turnstile, gave me my half-crown or whatever it was in those days – probably it wasn't as much as that – and then I had to wait behind the turnstile for him. He'd go into the Gwladys Street, pay his money, and then come back and collect me. For some reason, we always used to get to the game about an hour and a half before kick-off, so I used to stand by the rail and watch the empty pitch for an hour and a half until the game started. At the end of the game we crossed Stanley Park and went to my grandmother's, who lived just on around the wireless waiting for the results, they weren't a bit interested in the wedding. That was on 4 March 1950. The semi-final was played at Maine Road, but unfortunately Liverpool won 2-0.

Dolly Kelly

Mixing With The Reds

I don't like going to Anfield – in fact, I've only ever been there twice. One of the games was a derby game a few years ago and I was stood in the Kop with Raymond. The game finished 0-0. During the game another Evertonian came and stood next to us for some moral support, but he needn't have bothered. Throughout the game there were no problems and no antagonism – where else other than Merseyside could

you go to a derby game and enjoy an atmosphere such as that, with fans mixing together and enjoying friendly banter and rivalry?

Steve Bretherton

Harry Catterick's Broad Smile

When my parents celebrated their twenty-fifth wedding anniversary, we all went down to the restaurant in the old Liverpool airport. We were a party of about fourteen, and there was a large table all set out for us. There was also another table laid out, right at the top of the restaurant for about thirty people. We wondered who this large party could be, and began making speculations. In fact, it turned out to be quite a guessing game that night. Our speculation was soon over, when it was

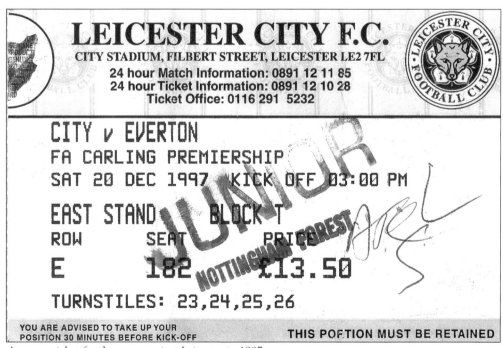

An away ticket for the game against Leicester in 1997.

A loyal supporter – aged three!

announced that the flight from London had arrived. A few minutes later the players and officials from the Everton team were seating themselves at the table. Harry Catterick had a broad smile on his face, so we assumed that they had won. Everything went fine for the first ten minutes or so, and then one or two of the players seemed to get a little boisterous. The odd pea was fired across the table, then there was a potato thrown, and finally, one of the players actually flung a piece of steak across the table. Although we had a very pleasant evening, the memory which is uppermost in my mind is seeing a piece of steak flying over the table.

Heather Jarvis

Do you Want any Tea Bags?

When I met the lads last week to go to the derby, we went into the St Hilda's. It's a pub that we've gone to for years. A good mate of ours was there, he works for MGM. When all their films are released in England, this chap's role is to sort out the distribution and marketing of the film. Naturally enough he meets lots of different people in his job, and there's lots of corporate hospitality to sort out. Anyway, on the first day of the season this year, when we were playing Aston Villa at home, he had to pick up this high-powered Villa fan and take him along to the game. Well, this chap was used to the full works. However, before they moved into corporate hospitality mode, my mate decided to take this chap along to the St Hilda's for a quick pint. It's not exactly the best pub in town, but it's quite acceptable before the game. Anyway, there they were in the pub, and this chap was not quite at his ease. And, to make matters worse, when he happened to be alone at one point during the proceedings, he was approached by some guy who was selling 'knock-off' shoes. The corporate hospitality guy just didn't know how to handle this situation. But more was to come. Sensing that a deal was being struck, an old woman who was sat over in the far corner of the pub sidled up to him and asked if he wanted to buy any tea bags – the best you can get, and only a pound for a hundred. Just in time, our corporate friend was rescued – but he'd certainly had an introduction to certain aspects of Scouse behaviour.

Tony Riley

Supporters' Club In Llandudno

My dad had a brother, Joey, and he lived and worked in Llandudno. He worked in the George Hotel, and some of the other big hotels around there. In Llandudno, I don't know whether you're aware of it, but they've got a good Everton supporters' club there, so they all used to meet in a pub called the St Tudno which is on the main street. Whenever Everton were playing, no matter where they were playing, there was a coach from the supporters' club. Understandably, the boot of the coach was completely full of beer. Whenever there was a home match, our Joe would meet all his brothers who still lived in Liverpool. They always met in the same pub before the match, because whenever Everton were at home, they always knew that Joe would be on the coach.

Dolly Kelly

Three keen Evertonians on holiday in Portugal.

Entertaining the Icelanders

Everton were playing against a team from Iceland called Keflavic. In those days I was a very keen and aspirant footballer myself. We trained before watching the match, and then we ran the six miles to the ground. In those days, with an Icelandic team, there was always the possibility of a heavy win. So we went into the ground, and stood watching our team. Before too long Everton scored. We were absolutely thrilled and delirious, and started jumping up and down. But, all the people around us stayed on their spots, and didn't move a muscle. It was only then that it dawned on us that we were in the Icelandic section of the ground. People were always very friendly on the terraces then, and we struck up a marvellous conversation with these Icelandic supporters. Next they started to produce all sorts of little fish delicacies which we'd never seen or tasted before. We started to talk about the game, who the best players were, how it was different in their country, etc. The whole event couldn't have been better. We even exchanged addresses with one or two of them. When our opposition did score, we gave them a good round of applause. When the game was over, Everton won 6-2; we shared a few drinks with them. They then boarded their coaches for the start of the long journey home, and we ran off into the night air for the six-mile jog home.

Nick Hawkins

'How Did Everton Get on?

When I was a child we lived with my grandma and granddad, and they lived in Lancaster Street, Kirkdale, so that's not far from both grounds. And I can remember my granddad when he was an old man and he was sick, sitting in his rocking chair. There was nothing on the wireless until the latest scores came out. And our Joe would be there marking his coupons off, and nobody dare speak whilst he was engaged in this delicate operation. When all the men were coming back from the match, my granddad would shout to them, and ask what the score had been that afternoon. 'How did Everton get on mate?' and they'd shout the score up. 'That will do me,' he'd say, and then he'd go in. He only wanted the Everton score. He didn't want to know about Liverpool. Strange to say, the year before he died, Liverpool started doing well; before that, Liverpool were nothing – they were in the Second Division. People said that they would get the cup that year. But my granddad said, 'Not while I'm alive will Liverpool get the cup' – and they didn't!

Dolly Kelly

The Pie Burst in my Pocket

I remember getting a meat pie at Everton, it was the first time that I went in the stands at Goodison. My dad took me as a special treat – he was in the Merchant Navy and had just come home from America. I had a new overcoat on – I was still in short trousers at the time – and he bought me this

A ticket for Derby County v. Everton.

meat pie. I put the pie in my pocket before climbing up to the stands. I really thought that I was going to fall out of them because they were that high. The pie burst in my pocket. It was one of the old pies which had the jelly on the top. We tried to get everything cleaned up, as my dad was concerned as to what my mum would have to say about my new overcoat.

Stan Cain

Another New Word

The first match that I ever went to was when I was seven. I think that it was a midweek match against Manchester United, and that it was a 1-1 draw. But the match itself caused me problems for weeks afterwards. During the game, everyone around me was using this new word – the 'F word'.

Being seven I didn't know what it was, although I did have some idea that you weren't allowed to say it. But, because it was a new word, I was saying it in every sentence. I used it in school; at home; in the street, and just about anywhere else that I could fit it in. So, my first memory of Everton is getting battered for weeks to come because of that word!

Paul Lucas

The Story Started to Unfold

One son's an Evertonian, and one son's a Liverpudlian, so ten years ago I went along to Villa Park to watch us beat Norwich. My other son went to Hillsborough. As we came out of the ground we started to get snatches of what had happened, and of course when we got back to the car we switched the radio on, and the story started to unfold

Terrance Harkin when he was a bit younger – he's now fifteen and a season ticket holder.

– you can imagine that we had mixed emotions on that day. I just had to find a phone box and phone my wife who was at home – I knew that my son was in the Leppings Lane end. I found out that he was OK which was a tremendous relief – he'd been able to use a phone from quite near to the ground and tell my wife that he was safe and well. I'll never forget that day, we'd come out on a high, but it was a very different story over in Sheffield. I always remember, he'd been carrying a Mars bar and it was absolutely flattened in the crush. That was a day of very mixed emotions, and I can understand the Liverpudlians losing interest in that particular competition, and maybe for slightly different reasons, I suppose we did as well.

Malcolm Hadwin

Beating the Old Enemy

Dean played for his country as well as Everton. He played against Scotland, the old enemy, on many occasions. The old man used to tell me that Dean was the first English centre forward to score two goals to beat Scotland at Hampden Park. Strange to say, the next centre forward to do it was Tommy Lawton.

Larry Lynch

Shouting for Everton

My younger brother was a strong Liverpudlian, but my mum and dad were staunch Evertonians. Sometimes on Saturdays the atmosphere in our house could be cut with a knife –

124

especially if there was a derby game. This situation went on for season after season until one day I suddenly realized that John was now shouting for Everton. I just couldn't understand this, because he'd been a Liverpool supporter ever since I could remember. When I tackled him on the subject he just passed it off by saying that he now realized that Everton were in fact the better team. The real truth came out years later however when I was chatting with my dad at a family party. What had really happened, was that my dad was so exasperated with John's allegiance to Liverpool that he issued an ultimatum – until he started to support Everton his pocket money would be stopped. Within days he was a proud supporter of Everton, and has been ever since.

Heather Jarvis

Grandma's Dog Called Dixie

Whenever we had a cat or a dog at my grandma's it was always called Dixie. My uncles and brothers were all merchant seamen, and whenever they were home on leave they'd come around and throw down a bone or some other scrap, and say, 'Here, give that to Dixie.' Even the cups in our house were all blue and white stripes.

Dolly Kelly

I Ripped my Trousers

We used to get into the Boys Pen and jump over into the ground. I was then able to stand behind the goal

alongside my dad. Well, with having short trousers, a rail caught my trousers as I was jumping over. It ripped my trousers, but fortunately dad had a pin, and he tacked me up.

Stan Cain

Lapsed Back into Unconsciousness

My brother, Peter Chamberlain, was an ardent Evertonian. Even as a youngster he was always good at football, so it came as no surprise when Cliff Britton signed him as an Everton colt. He made good progress, but unfortunately wasn't quite good enough

I walked up and down this road from nine o'clock in the morning until just before Gordon West arrived.

to make the first team. He later went on to play for both Swindon and Leicester. It was sometime during his playing career he was required to do National Service. Whilst he was out in Egypt that he was hit by a sniper's bullet. He was rushed to the local hospital, where he was unconscious for some considerable time. When he eventually did come round late one Saturday afternoon, he enquired about the Everton score. He was told that they'd lost – this precipitated his lapse back into unconsciousness!

Valerie Grue

Gordon West – Here Today

Years ago I met the great Gordon West – I was only seven at the time. My uncle was the manager at Tesco's just by the Black Bull in Walton. Gordon West was doing some promotion work there. My uncle got me to wear an Everton kit and walk up and down the street carrying this huge banner. The caption on it stated 'Gordon West – here today at 2.30'. I walked up and down this road from nine o'clock in the morning until just before he arrived. And, because my uncle was manager of the shop, I didn't get a penny for my efforts!

Steve Bretherton

What a Surprise

I've had a season ticket at Goodison for years and years. One season, the seat next to me happened to be vacant at the start of the season. As I wanted another ticket so that my son could go to matches with me, I made some enquiries at the ticket office, but was told that the seat had been sold. At the next home game, the seat was empty once again. In fact, the seat was empty at every home match right up until early December. By this time I was beside myself, having checked a few times with the ticket office, only to be told on every occasion that the seat had been sold. Anyway, at the first home game in December there was a chap sitting next to me in what had been the empty seat. I asked him why he hadn't been to all of the other matches. Somewhat sheepishly he confessed that his wife had bought a season ticket as a surprise birthday present – but hadn't given him the ticket until his birthday in December!

Frank Patterson

The Only Time I Went with Dad

The only match that I ever went to with my father, he supported Liverpool, was when we went to one match on a Boxing Day at Goodison when Hickson scored the only goal. We beat Bolton Wanderers 1-0. I saw Hickson, years later, and he looked a bit confused when I told him about this as I was shaking his hand. As I say, that's the only match that I ever went to with my dad, and it still sticks out in my memory.

Peter Spear

Roxann Farrell – a true Blue, aged four.

More Interested in United

I first started to watch Everton years ago when I was first married. I wasn't that interested in football at the time. But, as my new husband was going to be away from home every other Saturday afternoon during the season, I decided that it was better to go along to the game with him, rather than sit at home on my own all afternoon. Over the years I began to enjoy and understand the game more and more. My husband died a few years ago, but I still go along to the game. Where my husband used to sit, there's now another guy sitting next to me. He's quite a friendly sort of chap, but I'm not at all sure whether or not he's interested in watching Everton. As soon as the game starts he plugs in the ear-piece to his walkman, and then listens to either the Liverpool game or the Manchester United game – I'm sure that he's more interested in the United game.

Sally Greene

I Was Given a Final Warning

I used to work at AC Delco, and the foreman was a Liverpool supporter. I needed to go to the away games which were often on a Wednesday evening. I used to make up some excuses such as having an appointment with the dentist. It worked OK a few times, but when I started to go to the dentist on a regular basis, the foreman was surprised that I still had any teeth left in my mouth! When the dentist excuse was wearing a little thin, I used to say that I was going for an appointment at the hospital, and then I'd have to go into work with a limp. It wasn't too long before everyone realized that I was going to the away games rather than going to the dentist or to the hospital. I was given a final warning at work, but it still didn't stop me from going to away matches!